POLICY AND PRACTICE IN HEAL1

NUMBER FOUR

Service User and Carer Involvement:
Beyond Good Intentions

POLICY AND PRACTICE IN HEALTH AND SOCIAL CARE

POLICY AND PRACTICE IN HEALTH AND SOCIAL CARE
SERIES EDITORS
JOYCE CAVAYE and ALISON PETCH

Service User and Carer Involvement: Beyond Good Intentions

Edited by

Mo McPhail

*Staff Tutor, Faculty of Health and Social Care
The Open University in Scotland*

DUNEDIN ACADEMIC PRESS
EDINBURGH

Published by
Dunedin Academic Press Ltd
Hudson House
8 Albany Street
Edinburgh EH1 3QB
Scotland

ISBN: 978-1-903765-63-0
ISSN: 1750-1407

British Library Cataloguing in Publication data
A catalogue record for this book is available from the British Library

Typeset by Makar Publishing Production
Printed and bound in Great Britain by Cromwell Press

Contents

Series Editors' Introduction

It is a truism that the principle of involving service users and carers should be at the heart of policy and practice in health and social care. Indeed practice is unlikely to have long-term impact unless it is responsive to the voices of those at whom it is directed. The implementation of the principle, however, often proves problematic. Commitment to the principle can vary widely across different agencies and between different professionals within those agencies. Translation into practice can range from sophisticated partnerships designed to sustain long term involvement and influence to thinly veiled examples of tokenism, more concerned with 'ticking the box' than with genuine influence. Involvement, however, is also multi-faceted. It needs to respond to different levels of capacity and to allow for the introduction of innovation and experiment. More sophisticated models for involvement recognise this complexity and maximise the opportunities to embrace change.

This volume recognises this challenge in its title, 'Beyond Good Intentions'. The authors drew on their experience of participation, from a range of perspectives, during a two-year project which addressed user and carer involvement in social work education. In this book they set this experience within the broader context of other developments in the UK and develop a thoughtful analysis of how effective user and carer involvement can best be accomplished. The analysis is infinitely more valuable because it presents the voices of those different perspectives: the user, the carer, the educator. It was a brave decision of the team to explore and write about these different perspectives and the authors do not seek to gloss over some of the challenges they encountered. We are the wiser for them having brought their reflections together in this volume.

Dr Joyce Cavaye
Faculty of Health and Social Care,
The Open University in Scotland,
Edinburgh

Professor Alison Petch
Director, **research in practice for**
adults*, Dartington Hall Trust, Totnes,*
Devon

Glossary of Abbreviations

CCETSW	Central Council for the Education and Training of Social Workers
CU Group	Carers and Users Group (also referred to as the Users and Carers Group), Dundee University
SCIE	Social Care Institute for Excellence
SIESWE	Scottish Institute for Excellence in Social Work Education

"It's a mystery tour, but usually it just goes round in circles."
Cartoon by Richard Norris, reproduced by permisssion.

CHAPTER 1

Introduction:
Good Intentions in a Messy World

Mo McPhail and Wendy Ager

The good intentions are evident. Calls to greater service user and carer involvement in both health and social care services in Scotland form a backdrop to service planning and delivery which is recognisable throughout the UK. It is, for example, a requirement of the new social work degrees across the UK that service users and carers are involved in the design and delivery of such programmes (Taylor *et al.*, 2006). Based on our experience over two years in a government-sponsored service user and carer project, working to push forward into the territory beyond good intentions, we encounter a messy world of mixed messages.

These mixed messages are explored in the context of two dominant approaches to service user and carer involvement and in relation to the enactment of power at the various sites of involvement: a consumerist or managerial approach, and a democratic approach based on civil rights. Despite the constraints and limitations of 'top-down' government initiatives, we present a positive case for what has been achieved in effecting significant influence of service users and carers in social work education. Within the wider field of research and practice across the UK and beyond, we explore the relationships and processes required for alliances between social work academics and service users and carers to influence social work education and practice, with the ultimate goal of improved services and quality of life for service users and carers.

Why the book?

'We' are a group comprising a service user consultant, a carer consultant and academics from three universities in Scotland, who worked together on a government-funded social work education project from 2003 to 2005. We are keen to grasp the opportunity to write about our individual and collective experiences to communicate what has been a powerful learning process. This is a unique opportunity to write about service user and carer involvement at and between local, institutional and national levels, from individual and group perspectives, and across personal, professional and academic domains. This co-authored book is the result of these deliberations.

The collective experience of writing this book has challenged us all in very different ways. As individuals and as a group, we have wrestled with the means by which we communicate our experience. We decided that the best way to achieve this was to support each other through a system of writing buddies. This was an iterative process, involving many drafts and redrafts. It was a time-consuming and frustrating process at times, but one which resulted in a strong sense of ownership of the wording of the final version. In practice the greater challenge lay in supporting colleagues relatively new to writing for academic publication, and in co-ordination of the themes across the book. The democratic collective approach did not always lend itself to production of a co-authored, edited volume where strong leadership and clear and decisive decision-making is a necessity. However, throughout the process we aimed to ensure clarity of purpose in this joint activity.

Why service user and carer involvement?

Service user and carer involvement both in health and social care and in social work education raises a number of debates. For example, a major issue relates to value for money: such involvement is a time-consuming and costly activity, therefore evidence of effective change needs to be produced to justify these investments. Yet if involvement is carried out in a superficial or tokenistic way, there is a danger of betrayal of trust and a risk of doing a great disservice to service users and carers. The work of Mayer and Timms (1970) serves to remind us of what social work with no service user involvement in the development of services would be like. Over 30 years ago, they conducted one of the first research studies of the views of people receiving social work services. The discourse of the time that 'the expert knows best' suggested that the service user would be unable to comprehend the scientific knowledge on which social work practice claimed to be based. The conclusions of the research charted a mismatch of expectations and a clash of perspectives between the people who used the social work service and the agency's social workers. The authors concluded that service users must be actively involved in exploring what are relevant and effective social work responses to their unique needs. The irony, over 30 years on, was that similar comments were voiced by service users and carers at two conferences organised in 2004 by the Scottish project (Project 3.3) on service user and carer involvement in social work education. Two comments from service users reflect themes of the need for improved communication, increased understanding and awareness:

> I wish social workers had the ears to hear what my heart is saying. (Service user, Scottish Institute of Excellence in Social Work Education [SIESWE], 2004).

> We [service users] have to tune into their [social workers'] language and the way they speak. (Service user, SIESWE, 2004).

There is a new agenda for involvement of service users and carers in social work education, which focuses on extending understanding of the 'experiences' and expectations of service users and carers. Levin (2004) states:

> The purpose of the agenda is to ensure that newly qualified social workers have a thorough understanding of the standards of practices, processes and outcomes that service users and carers want. (Levin, 2004, p. 8).

A shared understanding of the purpose of such partnerships is fundamental to determining effective practice, though this can prove to be elusive (Taylor *et al.*, 2006). A purpose of service user and carer involvement is to develop more responsive, integrated services for the benefit of service users and carers. From the Scottish experience, Ferguson (2005) identifies more specific benefits of service user and carer involvement to social work education. These are that social work lecturers have a greater appreciation of the needs and experiences of service users and carers; service users and carers have a greater understanding of the social work task and the needs of other service user groups; and a significant level of trust is created between university staff and users and carers. This should reflect a commitment to address issues of power and process. The involvement of service users and carers has the potential to transform the nature of the relationship between service users and carers with social work academics and practitioners on a basis of mutual benefit and a more equal power base.

Project background – how we came together

Our involvement in the Scottish project began in 2003, when the Scottish Institute of Social Work Excellence in Social Work Education (SIESWE) distributed government funding to raise standards in social work education in Scotland at the time of the development of the new social work degree at honours level. (The Social Care Institute for Excellence [SCIE] is the equivalent agency in England.) The Universities of Dundee and Stirling and the Open University in Scotland were successful in their bid to work together on a project on service user and carer involvement in social work education, known as Project 3.3.

There was a strong sense of collective responsibility within the project management team from the start, which on reflection was a significant factor in the way the work of the project developed. Early in the project Norma McSloy and John Dow were appointed as carer and service user consultants, contracted on the same terms and conditions as a visiting lecturer. They provided a strategic link between the consultative service user and carer group at the University of Dundee and the development of a network at a

Scotland-wide level. Maggie Gee from the University of Dundee provided leadership and management of the project, Wendy Ager was appointed as the project development worker, Iain Ferguson from the University of Stirling undertook evaluation work, and Mo McPhail had the lead academic responsibility for developing a Scottish network of service users and carers in social work education. Our task was 'to explore a range of ways in which employers and people that use services and their carers can be involved in and contribute to the assessment process' (SIESWE, 2003).

The project was required to produce a number of outcomes linked to assessment in social work education. These included an audit of stakeholder involvement in social work education (Ager and Gee, 2004), the evaluation of a demonstration project and pilot projects to develop a framework of best practice for service user and carer involvement (Ager, 2004; Ferguson, 2005; Gee 2005; Ager et al., 2006), and finally setting up a national group of service users and carers as a reference group for SIESWE. This last task changed, by agreement, into working towards creating a Scottish national group of service users and carers involved in social work education.

Perspective of the book

We believe a rich area for exploration is a focus on the 'enactment of power' in policies and practices at and between national, institutional and individual levels and in the generation of social work knowledge. This requires a consideration of sources of power and the responsible exercise of that power to avoid tokenistic practice. However good the good intentions are, our experience is that they can so easily slip into tokenistic practice at each of these levels. The Oxford Dictionary of English (2005) definition of tokenism is:

> The practice of making only a perfunctory or symbolic effort to do a particular thing, especially in recruiting a number of people from under-represented groups in order to give the appearance of sexual or racial equality.

Tokenistic approaches to service user and carer involvement may additionally reflect approaches to inclusion of a range of minority groups within service user and carer involvement activities. At a global level parallels can be drawn between the way that professionals work with service users and carers and the way that northern nations work with southern nations. Professor Abye Tasse of Addis Ababa University shared his thoughts on this theme at the annual Joint Social Work Education Conference in 2005. He spoke about his experience of being a member of a social work department in a southern nation in receipt of aid from northern nations. He noted that difficulties could arise because of the domination and power of northern donor countries. Aid is given on their terms, using their knowledge and often planned without recourse to the depth of local networks that have full understanding of the recipient nation. The language is of co-operation but the power differential between north and south means that it does not work in an equal way. Northern nations benefit from being internationalised amongst themselves, sharing and exchanging expertise, but southern nations need to 'indigenise', to build on their own grassroots networks and knowledge.

There is a parallel here in the contrast between securely funded university social work staff, social work practitioners and institutions on the one hand, and on the other, service users and carers in that different country described by Norma McSloy as 'serviceland – a country within a country'. Service user groups, local and national, need strong and supportive networks that can operate independently alongside universities. Universities must seek to negotiate terms with service users, rather than directing the involvement themselves.

Structure and overview of the book

This introductory chapter sets the scene for the development of the book, introduces the Scottish project and considers the significance of service user and carer involvement. The first chapter, written by Wendy Ager and Mo McPhail, seeks to highlight the relationship and relevance of this project to other studies across the UK. Findings and themes from the Scottish project contrast with and complement relevant studies across England, Wales and Northern Ireland and further afield (Carr, 2004; Levin, 2004; Taylor *et al.*, 2006; Barnes *et al.*, 2006; Branfield *et al.*, 2006; Crisp *et al.*, 2006). Chapter 2, by Maggie Gee and Mo McPhail, focuses on two examples of processes to involve service users and carers in social work education, one within a university and one at national level. These link to work on the Scottish project and identify the achievements made despite constraints and competing approaches. In Chapters 3 and 4, carer consultant Norma McSloy and service user consultant John Dow powerfully reflect personal challenges posed by their experiences of a range of professional services, including social work education. They reflect on their experience of power differentials in practice, in a university context and at a national level. In Chapter 5, Iain Ferguson and Wendy Ager draw on recent messages from research and design of teaching and learning to examine the contribution that service users and carers can make to social work knowledge. In the final chapter we draw the main themes together and make recommendations for future development and service user and carer influence in professional education and training.

A final note on language and terms used

A focus in these chapters is on the enactment of power in relation to people who use services and carers, with language the touchstone in understanding the interlocking relationships. Montgomery (1995) signals the centrality of language in its all-encompassing function of informing 'the way we think, the way we experience and the way we interact with each other' (p. 251). Because it is an essential part of our lives together, it may fade in significance through familiarity and in the 'common sense' view that words are words, to be taken at face value. We adopt a more critical stance which proposes that 'the way language we use in talking about the world around us ... is active in constructing the world' (Forbat, 2005, p. 6). The interpretation and enactment of power, reflected in the use of language, is a key concept for the project team in making sense of this experience. It makes sense to lay down some definitions at an early stage. Swift provides an inclusive term to describe service users as:

> those who are eligible to access social work services – but [they] also include those who define themselves as potential users of social work services, either because they anticipate a future need, or because they choose not to use the services which are currently available to them. (Swift, 2002, p.19)

The term 'carer' is also contested, as many carers do not identify with the label of carer and there is no simple definition to distinguish different care relationships. The term 'carer' is often used interchangeably across the literature to refer to family carers, informal carers, paid and unpaid carers. Levin shares one definition: 'carers look after family members, partners or friends in need of help because they are ill, frail or have a disability' (Levin, 2004, p. 21). However, she argues that definitions should be discussed in the context of the group to reach a broad and acceptable definition. We have also experienced differing approaches to representation of service users and carers: some university groups choose to separate these service user and carer groups while others believe there is a shared perspective in relation to social work education, and seek to avoid labels. Many words are sprinkled liberally across the literature and government policy in this area, such as 'partnership', 'involvement', 'participation', 'collaboration', 'empowerment.' We use these terms with caution, guided by the sentiments of Braye (2000), that it is the intended meaning behind the action which is pertinent.

CHAPTER 2

Issues of Power in Service User and Carer Involvement: Partnership, Processes and Outcomes

Wendy Ager and Mo McPhail

Partnership is about managing power; it requires constant attention and is always work in progress. (Taylor *et al.*, 2006, p.103)

Our experience of partnership working on a Scottish project on service user and carer involvement in social work education has been a deeply politicising one. First-hand encounters with power enacted at various sites of service user and carer involvement across national, institutional and local university levels have demonstrated to us that 'partnership working that pushes at the orthodox structures of power is difficult' (Barnes *et al.*, 2006, p. 434). In this chapter we provide a commentary on service user and carer involvement in social services work, in social work education in particular, with a focus on the enactment of power. We explore the nature of partnership arrangements with service users and carers; examine the processes through which partnerships are navigated; and review what is known about the outcomes of such partnerships on social work knowledge and education, and ultimately on social work practice itself.

Understanding partnership with service users and carers in social work practice.

Our intention here is to trace the development and interpretation of service user and carer involvement in broad terms and to explore one recent policy in more detail as an example of government discourse, where we consider the language used and how this reflects relative power relations. The review of social work services in Scotland, *Changing Lives* (Scottish Executive, 2006), envisages 'real influence' (p. 9) being exerted by service users and carers at individual, operational and strategic levels. Other examples of recent service user and carer policy initiatives in social work education are summarised by Taylor *et al.* (2006), and include the Quality Assurance Agency's Benchmark Statements for Social Work Education (1999), the National Occupational Standards for Social Work and the frameworks for the new degree in social work in the UK.

There is recognition (Braye, 2000) that service user and carer involvement has developed over the years as a result of disparate and sometimes contradictory legal, professional and political drivers. Legislation concerning various groups – for example, children and young people (The Children Act 1989, The Children (Scotland) Act 1995); mental health (Mental Health (Care and Treatment) (Scotland) Act 2003); community care (NHS and Community Care Act 1990, Community Care (Direct Payments) Act 1996, Community Care and Health (Scotland) Act 2002) – and the Carers (Recognition and Services) Act 1995, which recognised the rights of carers over the last 30 years, have directed that the participation of service users and carers is an essential part of the provision of services. Some legislation is underpinned by wider European policy such as the European Convention on Human Rights and Fundamental Freedoms, incorporated into UK law by the Human Rights Act 1998, and by the UN Convention on the Rights of the Child.

Simultaneous developments have been spearheaded by user-led disability organisations, radical social services professionals and models of practice introduced with greater emphasis on ideas of citizenship and equality. These emerged as powerful forces for change (Beresford, 1993). Service users and carers have increasingly asserted their needs and rights as citizens to challenge ideologies and models of social care practice that pathologise rather than empower them. Taylor *et al.* (2006) note how the new policy requirements to involve service users and carers stem both from this anti-oppressive, rights-based agenda and the increased emphasis on managerial, consumerist approaches in social care services. Managerialism is defined as:

> an overarching set of changes introduced in the UK from the 1980s onwards that involves providing effective services at lower cost through application of management techniques borrowed from business and industry. (Waine and Henderson, 2003, p. 51)

It is a contested term and we explore some of the issues arising from this.

Ways of thinking about service user and carer involvement

Two common themes run across studies on forces fostering the development of service user and carer involvement. One is the 'consumerist, managerial' agenda of governments and the other is the agendas of various civil rights and social movements (Beresford and Croft, 1993, 2003; Pithouse and Williamson (1997); Kemshall and Littlechild, 2000; Powell, 2001; Harris, 2003; Taylor *et al.*, 2006; Cowden and Singh, 2007). The Conservative government's commitment in the 1980s and early 1990s to a free market philosophy placed great emphasis on the individual as a 'consumer' (Beresford, 1993). The notion of service user as consumer is robustly critiqued by Harris (2003), who states, for example:

Social work services users are not the affluent, identity-enhancing customers of the consumerist rhetoric ... they are turning to the state because they are unable to turn to the market as individual customers in their own right. (p.152)

The modernising agenda of the 1997 New Labour government continued in this general direction and sought to strengthen the participation of service users and carers in health and social care across the UK. Harris contends that, although New Labour sought to distance itself from both the New Right and Old Labour, it 'maintained its support for the bi-partisan consensus or state-sponsored consumerism that had developed in the early 1990s' (Harris, 2003, p.135), based on what he considers a flawed concept of service users as consumers.

'Consumerist/managerial' approaches and the 'democratic' approach have radically different implications. They may be seen to represent opposite ends of the continuum of models of service user and carer involvement. The consumerist/ managerial approach, associated with government or state service initiatives that are top-down, is concerned with improving efficiency and cost effectiveness and focusing on the individual consumer's rights and choices. The democratic approach is located in a very different political philosophy, with an emphasis on human and civil rights, citizenship, collective change and a social model of disability. The latter tends to be characterised by user- and carer-led initiatives and acknowledges that issues of power are central to the understanding of this arena (Beresford and Croft, 2003). Cowden and Singh (2007) also identify the consequences of developing a response to service users as consumers of services in contrast to the political left's more radical agenda of involving service users in emancipatory politics, challenging both political establishment and professional power. Taylor *et al.*, (2006) ask whether these perspectives can successfully be married to achieve effective outcomes in professional education.

How do these different ways of thinking about service user and carer involvement impact on service users and carers and practitioners? Braye (2000) suggests that, despite the fundamental contradiction between the two approaches, there is usually sufficient overlap to allow people with very different perspectives room to manoeuvre to work together relatively productively. That said, it is not always a comfortable position. In the Scottish project, particularly in work to develop a national network of service users and carers in social work, this tension was keenly felt and manifest in a number of arenas, discussed in more detail in Chapter 2. A continual challenge throughout the project was to maintain a solid link with the grassroots network philosophy and practice comprehensively discussed by Ager *et al.* (2005), whilst balancing the need to work to a tight budget and timetable set by others.

Such tensions have been noted elsewhere. Postle and Beresford (2007), for example, found that social workers faced considerable challenges in trying to implement approaches based on principles of citizenship in an environment which is dominated by managerial pressures. They describe the importance of celebrating achievements of service user campaigning groups to bolster enthusiasm and continued motivation. This resonates strongly with the experience of the Scottish project. Involvement was sustained because of shared purpose, shared information and shared decision-making as a team, as well as positive social contact between us. Such work requires considerable tenacity, high levels of commitment and motivation. By way of illustration of the complex and contested nature of such involvement, we now consider a particular government policy in greater depth.

The Scottish policy context of social work

The aspirational position of service user and carer involvement in social work for the next generation in Scotland is conveyed in the document *Changing Lives* (Scottish Executive, 2006), a report commissioned by the Scottish Executive to review the country's social work service in the 21st century. Although the policy is a Scottish one, we believe that the issues identified here and the broad learning is applicable across the UK.

Changing Lives envisages greater involvement of service users and carers in decisions about their own care and in the design and delivery of services. As an example of current thinking on policy and service development, it therefore provides an opportunity to examine the predominant discourse used to frame future developments in service user and carer involvement in Scotland. *Changing Lives* refers to those using social work services and people in a caring role as 'people who use services' and 'carers'. No definitions are given about these terms, in contrast to the detailed explanations provided regarding 'social work services, social workers and the social service workforce' (p. 7). This omission creates the impression that such terms are self-explanatory, part of received wisdom in the world. It is, however, important 'to justify and account for the labels used to describe the people involved (because) important implications are carried by the terms' (Forbat, 2005, p. 12). The key point is that the lack of critical analysis in the report betrays a dominant narrative which reinforces 'roles and identities of people in care relationships (which) are "static" and "unidirectional" (Forbat, 2005, p. 12). Service users are service users. Carers are carers. Everyone knows what this means.

This largely undifferentiated approach unfolds throughout the report. It is seen as sufficient to 'emphasise the experience of being a user' (Forbes and Sashidharan, 1997, p. 496), not acknowledging the different groups of people who may use services and their varying perspectives. Only once do we see any distinction drawn between people who use services and carers. This occurs in the report's recommendations which include separate headings for 'people who use services; carers; social service workers; employing organisations; the general public; partner professions and agencies and political leaders' (Scottish Executive, 2006, pp. 15 and 16).

Looking in closer detail at the way people who engage with social work services are described in the report, a divergent range of identities are reflected. 'Vulnerable people' occupy one extreme of the spectrum and 'citizen leaders' the other, with 'active participants' occupying the middle ground. Describing people in these particular and distinct ways reflects differences in the relationship between social workers/social work services and people using those services. Ideas about vulnerability and exclusion, for example, focus on the role of the social worker in providing support and protection leading to independence. Active participants, however, are engaged in developing their own care, suggesting a partnership with social work services, and working together to identify resources. Citizen leadership 'means people having more of a say and taking more of a lead in planning services' (Scottish Executive, 2006, p. 5). *Changing Lives* encourages social work services to 'embed in practice a new approach to citizen leadership' (p. 68) based on principles of participation identified by the review's User and Carer Panel. This panel was convened along with other sub-groups to support the review group, and constituted a panel of people who use social work services: it included people with a variety of backgrounds, aiming to reflect the diversity of service user and carer groups in Scotland.

It is suggested that leadership can be demonstrated at individual, operational and strategic levels, such that people who use services and carers can have 'real influence' (p. 9) on services. The new legislation proposed by the report would also 'enshrine citizen leadership ... embed[ding] requirements for all providers to actively engage people in the design and delivery of services' (p. 76). How this is to be achieved is not clear. The User and Carer Panel stated that 'there needs to be a shift in power away from people who commission and provide services to service users and carers' (p. 33). However, it is difficult to see where the mechanisms for such a shift lie. Those who are 'vulnerable' are somehow to be empowered as 'citizen leaders' to shape the development of services. Their experience and insight of services is acknowledged, but there is little recognition of the transfer of power required that will equip those who are vulnerable to exert 'real influence'. The paradox is evident. The review is written on the terms of those inviting participation rather than those with a right to it and, as such, is a reflection of where power relations reside.

Beresford and Croft (1993) suggest three crucial aspects to achieving citizen involvement:

> The first is changing ourselves so that we are better equipped to participate and enable other people's participation. Second is developing more participatory processes and structures in agencies and organisations. Last is changing cultures and climates so that ...

people's involvement is essential and valued in the wider world. (pp. 15–16)

Firstly, Beresford and Croft (2003) challenge us to change ourselves. Translating this into the process here, this means that training in citizen leadership, for example, will have to include social work practitioners as well as service users and carers. Building everyone's capacity will be important to shift the balance of power. Secondly, more participatory processes and structures will need to be developed. The User and Carer Panel is one such structure, but this needs to be multiplied by other structures and processes in each and every social work organisation in Scotland. Thirdly, they require cultures and climates to be changed: this seems the hardest of the challenges. Carr (2007) picks up this debate, identifying lack of organisational responsiveness – indeed, extending to signs of resistance – as a critical issue of the moment. Sharing accountability and shaping services inherent in 'citizen leadership' will thus require significant movement for all parties, 'where the power distribution is recognised for what it is' (Baldwin and Sadd, 2006, p. 353).

The first newsletter from a Changing Lives implementation group (Scottish Executive, 2007) contains commentary from a reconstituted User and Carer Panel, signalling their role to assist in monitoring the implementation of Changing Lives. They end on a critical note, reflecting their frustration that one year on from the publication of the report there appears to be very little visible impact of the much heralded changes, and that many in the social service workforce in Scotland know little about the content of the report. It is a promising sign that the Panel has been retained and even more promising if the Panel can maintain an independent and critical voice in the implementation of the key recommendations.

Involvement of service users in social work education

There is a relatively long history of the involvement of service users in social work education. More than a decade ago, a report by CCETSW (Central Council for the Education of Social Workers) argued for a more active role for service users and carers in social work education (Beresford et al., 1994). Its authors identified patchy and uneven involvement of service users in social work education.

According to an audit of Scottish social work education providers in 2004, (Ager and Gee, 2004) many of the concerns identified in the 1994 report appear to remain. Service users and carers still reported limited involvement in social work education. Some involvement in teaching or course production was identified by the universities in the 2004 audit, though participation of service users and carers in governance of social work programmes was still limited. The narrow role of service users in social work education, mainly in the context of social work placements, seemed to be a continued feature, with some practice teachers reporting that they seek feedback from only one or two service users or carers. There is, of course, a world of difference in 'providing feedback' as opposed to active involvement in the assessment process. Issues of planning and timing of such feedback were identified in the Scottish audit as requiring further exploration.

Taylor *et al.* (2006) conducted a practice survey across England, Wales and Northern Ireland and reported that the bulk of user and carer involvement took place in a practice learning context. They found continuing issues about the time needed to build and maintain relationships, and reported wide-scale agreement on the need to involve service users and carers as early as possible in the process.

Further evidence on current practice is provided by Crisp *et al.* (2006). They too reported that service user and carer involvement in assessment, where it occurs, is mostly in the context of practice learning. Although there was an overall positive disposition to service user involvement, there seemed to be a wide range of understandings as to what this actually means. As with the Ager and Gee (2004) and Taylor *et al.* (2006) studies, they found a lack of clarity about what service users and carers were being asked to assess. What is actually being assessed? The popularity of the student, or other issues unrelated to assessment of the student? They concluded that wider organisational and professional change at the level of university governance is required if the involvement of stakeholders is to move beyond an 'add on' to existing practices.

It appears that the same trends of managerialism in service user and care involvement in social work services have been reflected in social work education across the UK. Through meticulous attention to minutes of professional regulatory meetings between the late 1980s and the early 2000s, Harris (2003) demonstrated that the dominant discourse has been transformed from one of anti-oppressive practice to one focused on business principles applied to the process of social work learning. We consider next the out-workings of this shift on social work programmes in the UK.

Partnerships with service users and carers in social work education

What do we know about partnerships with service users and carers in social work education? Taylor *et al.* (2006) were commissioned by SCIE to undertake a systematic knowledge review of teaching and learning of partnership in social work programmes. This included focus on service users and carers as stakeholder partners. We consider the nature of the 'contract' or relationship between service users, carers and academics and practitioners as pivotal to effective partnership practice. The findings of Taylor *et al.* (2006) in relation to teaching and learning of partnership was that there was 'conceptual hybridity' and confusion regarding the term. Like Levin (2004), who refers to the ambiguous and often interchangeable use of such terms as 'partnership' and 'participation', they found no clear definitions and very little grounding in theory, despite a strong commitment to partnership working as a philosophy and a value base. Student understanding of user and carer experiences, and challenging stereotypes and discrimination, were the main foci.

First of all we consider who are the service user and carer partners within this arena. We concur with the views of Braye (2000) that 'participation in social care provision will reflect the patterns of dominance, inequality and exclusion that are inherent in the structures of the wider society' (Braye, 2000, p. 12). This means that the particular groups in society that are least well represented are also likely to be less present in the service user and carer movement and forums. Taylor *et al.* (2006) found that there was a wide spread of service user and carer groups, including people who were involved with social work services on an involuntary basis. A further report commissioned by SCIE (Begum, 2006), highlights the continuing issues around the decreased participation of Black and Minority Ethnic users and carers in social work over the last 20 years. She challenges myths and misunderstandings about Black and Minority Ethnic participation, to argue that when properly facilitated and supported such participation is both desired and possible. She argues for the continued importance of embedding issues of race equality in mainstream service user development. A study by Warwick *et al.* (2006) demonstrates what is possible, with an example of the participation of a much neglected social group, young asylum seekers and refugees, to record their experiences, in methods of their own choice, for social work students to hear.

A continuing challenge is whether service users and carers are jointly represented or whether their needs are sufficiently distinct to warrant separate forums. The work of Stalker (2003) is relevant here. She presents a case for the consideration of service users and carers as an integral caring system to guard against the polarising of one group against the other, arguing that promotion of the needs and rights of one group does not necessarily undermine the needs and rights of the other group. Rather, she highlights the interdependence between the two groups. There are different views as to how this can be organised. In the context of the Scotland-wide network, a decision was made for a joint forum of service users and carers, with a requirement to proactively attend to conflicting interests when they arose.

Power and partnerships

Power dynamics are frequently acknowledged in the literature of service user and carer involvement. However, from our experience, this is the 'elephant' in the middle of the room, rarely discussed explicitly at government policy, senior management or institutional level. The work of Curran

(1997) is relevant to the discussion of partnership with service users and carers at all these levels. She considers dimensions of visible and non-visible power relations in decision-making processes, in how ideas and language are constructed, and through discursive practices linking power to knowledge. Again, this resonates with the experience of the project group at both local and national levels, both in the experience of power between institutional and project level and within local university structures. Carr (2003) refers to the myriads of ways, usually unintentional, where service users and carers are disempowered, through use of professional jargon and setting people up in roles for which they are either ill-prepared or untrained. Braye (2000) also suggests that professional and organisational power is derived from a number of sources and that its use requires vigilance by all involved in service user and carer partnership work.

This approach seems highly pertinent in consideration of the power dynamics between those in powerful positions in government, social work education and academia, working alongside service users and carers, who are often located in marginalised and relatively powerless social and personal situations. Both John Dow and Norma McSloy's accounts in this book attest to this interpretation, working at both a local university and a strategic national level. Further work by Carr strengthens this view that 'exclusionary structures, institutional practices and professional attitudes can affect the extent to which service users can influence change' (Carr, 2007, p. 267) She draws attention to the clash between increasingly apparent approaches based on consumerism and more democratic approaches. Citing the work of Tew (2005), she challenges the *'false institutionally imposed consensus'* that can exist in Western public institutions and calls for an open dialogue where power differences can be honestly discussed.

Management approaches to partnership working with service users and carers are key. Braye (2000) identifies that a significant factor in promoting participation is the commitment of those with power in organisations to fundamental change in the nature of the relationship with users and carers from one of exclusion and dependency to one of respected partners. She advocates a reflexive approach to management, which encourages critical reflection on the use of power and the way it is enacted at various sites of operation. Our experience reflects this, that the approach to power issues by management at the various interfaces – between government, institution and local project – is critical, yet rarely explicitly discussed. The Scottish project group benefited from the involvement of service user and carer consultants, who were able to draw on the support of the service user and carer group at Dundee University, and were linked into a much wider network of service users and carers. They acted as a strategic bridge between the national and local, supporting findings of Vodde and Gallant (2002).

In interrogation of the 'relations of involvement' a pertinent question is whether it is ever possible for a 'top-down' government initiative to develop forums and networks where service users and carers can adopt leadership roles and maintain their independence from funding bodies? The work of Newman *et al.* (2004) provides a useful framework on which to hang such questions. They found contradictions between policies which stress collaboration and partnership and other conflicting, more managerial practices. Commitment and prior experience of 'officials and citizen participants' are identified as factors which bring possibilities for some influence towards more inclusive practice. In the Scottish project a common experience of working in the voluntary sector and a shared commitment to collective approaches were clearly facilitating factors. We now consider processes in which these partnerships are played out.

Power and processes of involvement

> Process is as important as outcomes when new policies are implemented, if the individuals using services are to become participant and experience choice and control. (Seden, 2007, p. 2)

The nature of the relationships between service users and carers, social work academics and practitioners both shape and are shaped by the processes of involvement. Processes also significantly influence outcomes. In this section, we consider messages from the literature about processes which are more likely to facilitate effective involvement and avoid tokenistic practice. These include the negotiated value base of the work, gauging levels of participation, integrated approaches to involvement, networking at both grassroots and national level and critical issues of funding for sustainable development.

Values in action

The critical importance of a values-based approach and genuine power-sharing is highlighted across a number of studies (Levin, 2004; Ager, 2005; Barnes *et al.*, 2006; Beresford, 2006; Taylor *et al.*, 2006). Levin (2004) draws on the experience of the service user movement to promote the idea that everyone involved in the process of service user and carer involvement should agree 'a written protocol of values, principles and practices that is then owned and signed up to by all parties' (2004, p. 9). As a project team, we made frequent reference to principles of 'mutuality' and 'demonstrable trust', drawn from the work of Shemmings and Shemmings (1995), who advocate that 'the insights of the least powerful actors in social behaviour are as important as the most powerful' (p. 52). These concepts became touch-stones for testing the strength of relationships. In fact, frequent references to this work became part of the humour of the group and thus embedded into the culture of the project team. This approach is further reflected in the good practice principles for service user and carer involvement developed by the project team in relation to participation, teaching and learning in universities, practice learning, student assessment, governance and payment for involvement (SIESWE, 2006).

Levels of participation

We have deliberately used the generic term, service user and carer 'involvement', on the basis that levels of such involvement should not be taken for granted and require careful scrutiny. The ways in which service users and carers in social work programmes are involved reflects both relative power positions and personal preference. In one of the few studies to discuss recruitment of service users, Stevens and Tanner (2006) discuss the impact of methods of recruitment on the process, and recognise different preferences regarding levels and types of involvement. Levin (2004) identifies different models to gauge levels of participation (Arnstein, 1969; Goss and Miller, 1995 and Brooker, James and Readhead, 2003), noting a range of approaches by university and college social work programmes, from limited to integrated, and school-wide involvement. She charts the progress of involvement of service users from initial contact to strategic management. Ager and Gee (2004) draw on an adaptation of Arnstein's work to make sense of the nature and level of service user and carer work at the University of Dundee. Subsequently John Dow has become Chair of the Programme Committee and also Chair of the national group, Scottish Voices, meeting the criteria of delegated management and involvement in governance.

Levels and types of involvement are reflected in the varied discourse in the literature, describing service users and carers as co-trainers (Manthorpe, 2000), Citizens as Trainers (Boylan *et al.*, 2000), consumer teachers (Curran, 1997), and service users as teachers and advisers. Scheyett and McCarthy (2006) in the USA refer to a structured dialogue approach between users of mental health services and social work students, as modelling partnership and collaboration in a social work education setting. Our experience is that involvement of service users and carers in leadership roles at a strategic management level from the earliest stages is critical to the process of effective partnership working.

An integrated approach

Can sound partnership practice be developed on a piecemeal basis? Barnes *et al.* (2006) found that addressing issues of power in partnerships with service users and carers in a post-qualifying mental health programme was vital to the success of the partnership and that involvement of service users at the stages of commissioning, implementation and evaluation of a postgraduate programme in mental health training programme was critical. An impressive feature of this project is that where difficulties arose, the team did not back off from the involvement of service users; rather, every attempt was made to further equalise the power relationships. Careful consideration of the make-up of the programme's management board at policy-making level was identified as a key issue. Interestingly, they found very similar responses to service user involvement across the professional groupings, with student reports of improved knowledge and skills in partnership working and some, though limited, changes in organisational practices where students undertook their practice learning. Key learning here was about the importance of an integrated approach across the programme at all levels of participation and the need to address power-sharing practices honestly.

Networks – at grassroots and national level

Networking is considered to be a vital component of a strategy to address the power imbalance between service users and professional and academic organisations (Beresford and Croft, 2003; Branfield et al., 2006; Beresford and Branfield, 2006). We suggest that the further development of grassroots networks at local and regional level has the potential to counter centralising and controlling tendencies of top-down government initiatives. There is a growing understanding that grassroots networks can create 'social capital' (Barbera, 2005; Kovalainen, 2005). Social capital is a key resource for acquiring other resources including knowledge and power. Rosenkopf et al. (2001) examined organisational networks and found that informal networks were stronger amongst front-line staff than amongst senior executives. Contacts between workers, trade union members and professional or trade groupings provide effective ways of sharing information which may develop into new ideas to be fed upwards to a strategic level. Networking is increasingly being viewed as an effective means of establishing groupings that can challenge the power of established hierarchical structures. This approach used by service user and carer groups could be a formidable influence in social work education at national and at university level.

> The more we network, the more powerful we can become and the more united our voice will be. (Branfield et al., 2006, p. 4)

This view from a service user reflects key messages of a report written by a team from the national network of service users in England, Shaping Our Lives, on making user involvement work (Branfield et al., 2006). Branfield and her colleagues stress the importance of service user-led groups having a national voice which allows them to meet together for collective support, share information and protect against any inappropriate treatment or manipulation of service users in their work with university programmes. Collective approaches help to address potential isolation of individual service users and service user organisations, inadequate and insecure resources and a low profile. An adequately resourced user-led national network in social work education is seen as vital to sustain and develop more effective influence.

Funding

A fundamental principle is that service users and carers should be paid for the involvement work they undertake on behalf of social work education providers. Funding remains a problem in a number of ways. Significant difficulties arise, firstly from the amount of money people are allowed to earn without a negative impact on welfare benefits, and secondly from the complexity of information about what does and does not count as income. We return to this issue when we consider the factors that constrain involvement of service users and carers in social work education in Chapter 2.

Other areas of difficulty concern funding to universities for the development of service user and carer work. In Scotland, no additional resources have been made available. Social work colleagues in England and Wales, who received initial government financial support, are concerned about the long-term sustainability of involvement work without dedicated resources (Levin, 2004). Much additional work has been undertaken over and beyond normal duties, partly because of the commitment of individuals, service users and carers and academic colleagues. Without ring-fenced resources, sustainability of this work in the longer term is seriously threatened. Finally, financial systems in universities are severely challenged by the need to pay people who may not have bank accounts, and to pay them in a timely fashion. This is a considerable issue of power and is not yet resolved, despite the Department of Health report.

Agenda-setting

A key issue of power relates to agenda-setting. The agenda for service user and carer involvement in social work education in the UK is seen as largely led by the universities and government-funded 'centres of excellence' (Beresford, 2007). Much positive practice has developed as a result of these initiatives, which is to be applauded, reflecting the dedication and commitment of a large number of people in social work education and service user and carer allies. To sustain and further develop this work the strategic working of service users and carers at national, regional and local levels needs to be addressed (Branfield *et al.*, 2006, 2007). This resonates with our experience at a local and national level that, despite many positive developments, barriers to full and effective involvement remain. These include the patchy and variable levels of participation across the social work programmes; the power differences in valuing service user and carer knowledge; the culture and processes in many universities, which may be hostile to external involvement; and issues of training and funding to further develop the capacity of many service user and carer groups. In this context, it is important to consider the impact and outcomes of such work not only in social work education, but also in the developing sources of social work knowledge and ultimately in social work practice itself.

Influencing outcomes of social work education and social work knowledge

In the final section of this chapter we review research on the outcomes of service user and carer involvement, in terms of both social work education and social work knowledge. Ultimately an important consideration is to develop measures of the impact of service user and carer influence in social work practice. Knowing whether their involvement is making a difference to student social work learning and future practice is just as important to service users and carers involved in social work education as it is to social work academics, university and practice-based colleagues, policy-makers and professional and funding bodies.

In 2004, monitoring, review and evaluation of service user and carer involvement in social work education were described in terms of an impending task, to be done once the new social work degree was embedded. This is a current topic for debate. Levin (2004) writes, in her conclusions of the SCIE Resource Guide, of the need to gain understanding of the value of such involvement to processes and outcomes of social work education. Carr (2004) notes how little is known about outcome-focused evaluation, in the face of a preponderance of process-based evaluation. Taylor *et al.*(2006) also concluded that there were 'no overall conclusive findings reported on whether partnership work is effective for students' (p. 100). They did, however, note a number of studies where claims were made of positive changes in student attitudes and knowledge of partnership work with service users and carers, as opposed to demonstration of practice. Scheyett and Diehl (2004) also demonstrate evidence of positive student attitude change, although their work is not followed through into a practice setting.

In the evaluation of the Scottish project, Ferguson (2005) found similar changes in student attitudes, and that students appreciated and valued the experience of service users in relation to the project. It is regrettable that the evaluation was not extended to the development of the national group, which fell outside the remit of the SIESWE-funded project. The Scotland-wide network is now at a stage of commissioning a work programme. Drawing on learning from the first years of the implementation of the social work degree, it would seem appropriate to cost and undertake an integrated system of evaluation of outcomes of the work of the group at this key stage. Taylor *et al.* (2006) call for more extensive longitudinal research to 'explore the relationship between identified aims and outcomes and the development of good practice' (p. 104).

In view of the dearth of research on the impact of service user and carer involvement, the study by Barnes *et al.* (2006) makes a significant contribution. They undertook an evaluation of a five-year inter-professional mental health training programme. Their findings suggest that service user and carer involvement can be effective in developing knowledge and skills in partnership working, at individual and organisational levels, and to some extent changing student attitudes. They found the most influential area to be in relation to service user and carer involvement in teaching and learning. These claims are tempered with the statement that the researchers could not unambiguously attribute change to the involvement of service users. This would have required some form of control group against which comparisons could be made, though the authors suggest that their approach to evaluation could be used as a model to evaluate other such work. A strength of the Barnes *et al.* study is that it explicitly addresses power differentials in the structures and processes of the professional education context, recognising that this involvement can challenge the very foundations on which professional authority and knowledge is based.

Evidence regarding the outcomes of service user and carer involvement in social work education is currently tentative. What of evidence of its impact on social work knowledge? A number of studies have offered a qualified critique of the systematic knowledge review and evidence-based approaches utilised by the country-specific Care Councils of the UK. Fisher (2006) counsels caution in adopting an uncritical approach to the role of these organisations in developing 'excellence' in underpinning social work and social care knowledge. He concludes that otherwise definitions of the nature of knowledge will be too narrow and there is danger of 'ossification' of the relationship between knowledge and practice. Gray and McDonald (2006) also offer a critique of the approach of the 'Centres of Excellence', suggesting that there is a danger of employing too narrow a conceptual base. They advocate integration of ethical reasoning to enhance and better reflect the dynamic theory/practice link.

Humphreys (2005) reflects on the contested nature of what counts as knowledge, and the relationship between power and knowledge as applied to the social work education context. She challenges the notion of hierarchies of knowledge drawn from the medical world, and argues for the inclusion and valuing of service user and carer, organisational and community knowledge. Glasby and Beresford (2006) reinforce this, observing that the 'evidence-based' approach tends to be located in a medical model, rather than a social model. They suggest that experiences of people who work for and use social services are essential elements of such knowledge, to ensure a broader and more grounded view of the issues under consideration.

Conclusions

The enactment of power is a critical factor in the outworking of service user and carer involvement in social work, and specifically in social work education at every level and form of participation. This is evident in the discourse of service user and carer involvement in government policy; in the nature of partnership working, transmitted through the processes of involvement; and in the lack of attention to user-led outcomes of such involvement. The arena of social work knowledge is a further site where discourse of service user and carer involvement is contested.

We have noted that there is an overwhelming mandate for service user and carer involvement from legislation, professional values and service user and carer movements, but that this is often ill-defined and its mechanisms and funding are too uncertain for a more comprehensive realisation. The implementation of such work is best understood at and between national, institutional and local levels through the conceptual spectrum of managerial/ consumerist to service user and care-led democratic models. The emphasis on tight centralised control of managerial approaches, however, raises questions as to how much room there is for a greater sharing of the agenda for service user and carer involvement. We recognise the contradictions and tensions of attempting to implement more democratic ways of working in 'top-down' managerial contexts but also recognise the examples of good practice and potential that can emanate from such initiatives given the commitment and direction of those involved.

A combination of factors are identified which promote participation. These include a commitment of those in powerful positions to change the nature of the relationship; an explicit values-in-action, integrated approach; and a reflexive approach to decision-making and management. Evaluation of outcomes and the impact of such involvement is a much neglected area. This is a high priority and should help to address questions of whether effective change has been achieved. This is in everyone's interests. Above all, service user and carer involvement needs to be grounded and continually regenerated at grassroots level. We contend that grassroots networks at both local and national levels offer a key mediating function, countering the centralising tendencies of 'top-down' systems. Wider organisational and professional change is required if we are to go beyond good intentions and achieve sustainable and effective partnerships. A pressing concern is to ensure that the diverse communities of service users and carers are reflected across the web of networks and that the enactment of power is attended to at all these sites of involvement. In the next chapter a case study is presented of what can be constructively achieved despite the constraints and limitations outlined here.

CHAPTER 3

The Voice of Service Users and Carers in Universities

Maggie Gee and Mo McPhail

Transforming good intentions to involve service users and carers in the design and delivery of the new social work degree into effective practice at university and institutional level is a challenging process. In this chapter we consider how groups of service users and carers can influence and impact on these structures. We focus on the processes and outcomes of the Scottish project, exploring work carried out to establish both local and national mechanisms for service user and carer influence. Reflecting on our learning from these involvements, we note what hinders, but more importantly what helps, achieve service user and carer influence in social work education. Firstly we examine influence within a university through the case example of the University of Dundee, then we examine development work to set up a Scottish national network of service users and carers involved in social work education.

Having a voice and influence at the University of Dundee

Over a four-year period staff members at the University of Dundee have been involved in working with service user and carer experts by experience, amongst them co-authors of this book, to change the education of social workers of the future. We have worked to ensure that teaching is guided not just by researchers and practitioners but by those who know what it is like to receive services and who can say clearly what is most important to them. In 2003, service users and carers in the Department of Social Work, University of Dundee, had no role in governance of the department or in the assessment of social work students. Some were involved in teaching but this tended to be in specialist areas alongside social workers. In that year, 10 service users or carers contributed to teaching in the qualifying programmes for 160 students, which did not amount to much influence on strategy, students or staff.

Members of staff and practice teachers at Dundee sought a way in which they could engage with service users and carers on their terms. This was not easy because, to start with, we had to make connections. We believed we had to begin with service user and carer views rather than our own. Organisations were contacted that had some prior involvement with the teaching of social work students. These organisations had service user-led groups, and these groups had enough knowledge of social work training to contribute to the process. However, we did not direct or restrict involvement or develop quota systems from different groups. We wanted to allow the group to develop in its own way. Academics felt that they wielded enough power in social work education and must seek to stand back from unnecessary direction. From these groups some individuals agreed to come forward to be part of an initial 'CU' (carers and service users) Group. From the start this network development was ad hoc: rather than beginning with aims and constitutions we began with contacts and worked with who turned up. The strengths of grassroots networks lie in their access to individual views and actions but their informality and spontaneity may also work against a democratic approach (Koniordos, 2005).

It was with some trepidation that six people came to the first meeting with fears that this would be another tick-box token consultation with little likelihood of genuine outcomes. Service users and carers in the CU Group, such as Norma McSloy (Chapter 4) and John Dow (Chapter 3), noted that they had been 'consulted to death' by health boards and local authorities, yet little change had come from consultation (Ager *et al.*, 2005). The earliest meetings of this group were attended by between six and twelve service users/carers, a lecturer, two practitioners and occasional students.

Working to principles in the CU Group

We should note here that while CU stands for Carers and Users, there is also a touch of bravado in the phrase 'see you!' in Scotland. The CU Group started by agreeing the purpose of the group and then developing a way of working that was distinct from university committees or meetings. This distinctiveness is reflected in the six principles governing our way of working that were debated and refined in early meetings. These are that there must be:

- No tokenism. Representation should be purposeful, with genuine shared power.

- Fair funding. Where carers and service users teach, assess or represent, fees and expenses must be arranged.

- Consultation at grassroots level with groups of people who experience social workers and social work students in their daily lives. Representation should have its roots in such 'bottom-up' networks.

- Change from consultation. Systems of consultation must have end-products that are clear to service users and carers and that encourage a sharing of views.

- Plain English used wherever possible.
- A voice for all groups – including groups that are marginalised.

These ground-rules require meetings to be conducted in a manner understandable to all. We use plain English and have cards to show when a member wants to speak or cannot understand. The Chairperson, a service user, was selected for her quiet tact and firmness which helps in an occasionally rowdy meeting. There is no 'standing on ceremony' and after four years of operating, generally trust and good humour abound. Over time, trust and shared respect make meetings enjoyable for all and members are quick to comment on tokenistic use of time. The one academic who attends regularly has clear power in the process, but the positive environment engendered and the individual skills of representatives mean that service users and carers can be confident in challenging that power.

Funding CU work

We have ensured good administration to pay expenses and attendance fees, following the agreed principles of working. The Social Work Department in Dundee has allowed £20 per session, plus travel expenses, for service users and carers who contribute time to teaching, assessment and governance. However small this may be, we have found that all service users and carers value this gesture and feel that it gives recognition to their work. The lack of central government funding for involvement endangers all aspects of our work. Yet appeals to the Scottish Executive from Dundee, and indeed all other Scottish institutions involved in social work education, have so far been in vain. We are also currently working to ensure that these small amounts do not endanger the benefits received by individuals or create tax difficulties. Whilst guidance is available (Cooley and Lawrence, 2006) we have found that each individual situation is different and that university administrations have little capacity for complex systems.

The organisation and working of the CU Group

The CU Group has now met for four years about once every six weeks. Significantly, members define the group as a group of *influence*, not an advisory group (see Chapter 4). The intention of the group is to ensure that service user and carer views impact on social work education. Members 'represent' physical disabilities, learning disabilities and people with mental ill health, older people and people in the criminal justice system, young people, family carers and foster carers. However, members are clear that they do not 'represent' in an elected democratic way but as a trustee for the service user and carer groups with whom they have contact, informed by a range of collected views. We use formal systems, minutes, papers in advance and decisions by majority. Members agree that a group with intent to influence must be clear and transparent in its workings.

We debate issues, scrutinise proposals and generally further the influence of service users and carers on selection, teaching, governance and assessment processes of the social work qualifying programmes. We have developed a 'personspec' – a way of denoting the requirements and abilities needed for tasks asked of the group – so that members can work to strengths. The work of the CU Group can sound straightforward, and indeed relationships within the group mean that generally a consensual view is achieved, but here as elsewhere there are hierarchies of power present. The most articulate will make the most points, even when members use sign-cards to request to speak or request information. This mirrors the hierarchies within a university institution where those with high-level skills in academic communication, written or spoken, may direct those less skilled. It also mirrors the role many members take in service user organisations in the community, when they seek to speak up for other people disempowered in society. The aim of the group is to make sure marginalised voices, those of service users and carers, are heard in social work education. Group members have described it thus:

> What is needed is for the 'High Heid Yins' or the 'High Command' to get a sense of what being in the trenches is all about. After all, making decisions miles away from the action does not give a true picture of the realities and fears and concerns of the troops on the ground. (CU Group, 2005)

The CU Group has to ensure that the voices of service users and carers are heard and that service users and carers and academic representatives can be fairly confident and comfortable working together. From the beginning, members have not felt inclined to separate out service users and carers or to see these groups as different or competing. This may have been down to the counsel of early members, who did not see clear-cut boundaries between the two groups, and indeed we have members representing criminal justice service users and mental health service users who have caring responsibilities too. In addition, the divide between service users and carers, whilst clearly defined when debating local authority resources or within individual case conferences, is less defined in social work education.

The group also has to negotiate working expectations between its members and academic structures. The CU Group operates within a powerful institution and one in which authoritative members of the social work community are employed. It is not difficult to see that overt and covert power is exercised by staff, and that neither good intentions nor fair rules can counterbalance this when set against the often power*less* position of people who have a marginal place in the powerful hierarchy. A brief example may illustrate this. At the start of the development of the CU Group, disagreement arose between the CU Group and an academic management group over using the term 'bad social worker' in a questionnaire. The CU Group thought it was plain English, but it had to change the term because it was seen as a poor reflection on the profession by the professionals themselves. The academic management view prevailed. It taught the group a lesson that at the end of the day committees or individuals at the university have the power to overturn decisions made by the CU Group. Nevertheless, the CU Group continues to work alongside university representatives to ensure that the CU voice is heard. This is not easy for group members who may not have the knowledge and authority present in universities. However, they have tacit knowledge of how to work as less powerful partners, shaped over many years.

The wider network of service user organisations

Initial group members brought to meetings the names of organisations that might be interested in some sort of link with the university. These organisations were contacted and briefed, and some agreed to be linked to the university and to brief lecturers or CU representatives when required. They became the basis of a service user and carer grassroots network. John Dow, a founder member, envisaged the network as a delicate but enduring spider's web spun around the social work education programmes. Within the web, through diverse connections, are lecturers and service users and carers and their supporting groups, an interdependent rather than a hierarchical structure.

The CU Group debated and agreed a system of lecturers linking with service users and carers to gain a better sense of their points of view. The system requires lecturers to link every year to two service user and carer groups from the 40-strong network in a planned manner, with the process overseen by the CU Group. Meetings take place at a venue and time suited to the groups. These visits allow lecturers to connect with service users and carers for whose needs they train social workers. They have to think of their own skills, anxieties and preconceptions and work throughout the visit, linking what they hear to teaching strategies. When lecturers move out of their own environment into those of service users and carers, they lose some of their perceived power, which is taken up by the host service user or carer group. The information and ideas discussed are logged on a shared departmental file so that all lecturers can access them. The network of 40 groups supports CU members and gives them, if not a representative status, a means of referring back to others in the wider community.

What outcomes have been achieved from these linkages? As a result of one lecturer's visit, a group of five older service users helped to solve concerns surrounding younger students' anxieties – even dislike – about ageing and working with older people. They contributed to direct teaching and to video teaching and confronted the students with these concerns in class, in part by giving accounts of the positive aspects of their lives and in part by giving advice on communication skills. The dialogue between the class and the older people helped students to see that there was much more in common than different between the two groups.

The evaluation of the project also indicated positive benefits of those links (Ferguson, 2005):

> You did the visit; it was incredibly useful, not just in a 'that felt good' sense but clear applications to your teaching. (p. 11)

> I probably didn't really think of the service users and carers that much when I was doing my teaching ... I am much more in tune; I've read much more about service users and carers' programmes and rights and feelings and all the rest of it, in terms of articles, in a way I wouldn't have done before. (p. 10)

Service users and carers who had experienced these visits felt similarly positive:

> Very informative for everyone involved.

> In partnership, the tutor gave a very clear idea of what would be involved.

> The visit encouraged a lot of discussion.(Ferguson, 2005, p. 13)

Now the challenge is to maintain contacts and thus interest and enthusiasm for social work education that is influenced by service users and carers. A number of factors appear to impede this process. Not all lecturers choose to visit; other priorities get in the way, and despite taking this up formally the CU Group has found that it cannot force the issue. Perhaps one reason why some lecturers fail to engage in the process is that when making visits they are not on their own territory. They may feel their skills are rusty and their social work academic identity may be seen to stand on an ability to engage with service users and carers well. A second factor is lack of finance, which prevents a proposed service user development role that could work to strengthen the network and encourage visiting. Without central funding support for this area of work, the grassroots network subsides into the background, with potential rather than actual influence. Members still have links through student placements, teaching and a newsletter but this does not amount to the level of influence intended at the start. This is in comparison with the CU Group itself, which has flourished within the university, perhaps because resources and supports are adequate for its maintenance:

> Some of our members of the Group are extremely vulnerable and/or disabled but their enthusiasm and skill in passing on their specialised knowledge to students is an asset, we believe, beyond measure to the university. We should like to acknowledge, also, the hard work put in by staff members and the confidence the group has acquired through their extremely successful relationship building. (Elinor Dowson and CU Group members, 2007)

Ideas developed through service user and carer involvement: influencing management and policy

What kind of developments have the CU Group and the wider network initiated over the past four years? In terms of management and policy, CU members have been part of the development and management of the two new qualifying social work programmes. John Dow currently chairs the Programme Committee. This is an example of using members' talents appropriately. He, for example, has wide experience of meetings from earlier work. The second representative to this committee from the CU Group has experience of education. Both have the confidence to contribute and in the perceptions of staff add a quality to meetings that could be described as bringing into focus 'the people in the processes of social work and social work training'. John, as Chair, brought 'Service User and Carer Issues' and 'Student Issues' to the top of the agenda when he saw that they were marginalised at the end of the agenda when some staff had left. He noted with concern, however, that when he was absent from a meeting his re-ordering was momentarily lost.

New developments in teaching, action learning, video role-play and written work

Innovative use of service users and carers in teaching has increased. Prisoners contribute to teaching on criminal justice; a carer who leads regional developments on recovery in mental health gives input that counterbalances the strong input on the statutory role in this area delivered by mental health officers. Care leavers have contributed their opinions of social workers on video. Action Learning sets at the very start of the undergraduate programme send students out to the homes of a variety of service users and carers to listen to their views of social work and social workers and to gain a sense of individuals' lives before they start to develop a sense of their own professional stance with individual service users and carers. Students appear positive about this form of learning:

> We are benefiting from service users' experience.

> Before I visited the service user I did not take into account the emotional impact that some situations may have on me as a practitioner. (Comments by students, quoted by Gee, 2004, p. 3)

A further development at Dundee engages students in live videoed role-play with service users and carers. Postgraduates work with children and young people in the care system – the children particularly enjoy teaching students – and undergraduates work with adult service users and carers. Certainly students are very nervous but a large majority agree that there is key learning in this work and they are unanimous in recommending it be continued for future students. Comments from students include:

> They know better than anyone but they do not want to give criticism.

> I found it a really helpful thing to be part of as a service user – no one else really knows how it feels as a service user – I wanted to take the opportunity to show them. comment by service user (Comments by students, quoted by Gee, 2005, pp. 6 and 7).

Ager (2005) compared the extent and quality of service user and carer feedback in a sample of twenty practice learning reports taken from two cohorts of students in 2003 and 2004. These particular years were chosen as they represented a snapshot before and after a requirement for service user and carer feedback was put in place by the university. The content of these reports was examined, and practice teachers who had been involved in writing the reports were interviewed, to examine the impact of involvement on students' practice. There was – as might be expected, given the requirement – a significant difference in the extent of feedback evident in the reports in the two years sampled. Of the ten reports written in 2003, for example, six contained no feedback at all. By contrast, in 2004, all ten reports contained feedback from either people who use services or carers. However, when the quality of feedback across the two years was analysed, little discernible difference was to be found. In both 2003 and 2004, feedback was predominantly about the relationship established between student and service user or carer, and the communication between them. For example:

> The children's mother told me that the brother was shy of meeting the student, but his sister had told him the student was nice and easy to talk to. (Ager, 2005, p. 3)

Feedback is usually reported by the practice teacher, not directly quoting the person's own words. No examples of negative feedback were found. In mapping the feedback across the two years, no discernible difference was evident. Practice teachers' comments gave some reasons for this. They felt that more work was needed to enable students to understand what constitutes constructive feedback and to find creative methods of getting feedback in the diverse settings they are placed in. They also wanted guidance and 'tools' themselves, echoing findings elsewhere (Ager and Gee, 2004; Ramon et al., 2006).

There was, more significantly, a 'missing link' across all the reports. None of the students reflected on the feedback, on how it influenced their practice, or on how it fed into the assessment process. Neither did the practice teachers. Practice teachers commented on this lack of integration, suggesting that feedback may 'reinforce what students already know' or may sometimes indicate specific learning points. However, feedback was often found to be 'overwhelmingly positive', and indeed some practice teachers did not rate the quality of feedback as having anything worthwhile to offer:

Feedback hasn't a critical edge and so it can't be tested to any extent. (Ager and Gee, 2004).

Underlying this comment is the implication that other forms of feedback do have 'a critical edge' and therefore can be validated, or tested. These are presumably sources of professional feedback and point to power differences which show themselves in the 'asymmetry of meaning choices available to the powerful and less powerful' (Shirato and Yell, 2000, p. 142). This can also be detected in the lack of time devoted to collecting feedback. On the face of it, this appears to be a practical problem associated with the pressure of work in a busy placement. This seems, however, to indicate a lower priority to gathering feedback compared with supervision, training team meetings etc. A number of practice teachers acknowledged that seeking feedback was not usually an integral part of agency policy, so that for most people, seeking feedback is something students do to fulfill university requirements.

What conclusions do we draw from this exercise? Firstly, there is little evidence as yet of a shift in the influence service users and carers bring to bear on students' practice as a result of a requirement to include their feedback. It is pleasing to note the inclusion of feedback, but so much more can be achieved in this process to the benefit of students' practice. Secondly, there appears to be a continuing endorsement of 'the professional's' role, such that power relations are maintained on a 'professional–service user or carer' axis. Thirdly, just as Baldwin and Sadd (2006) found, 'agencies in which collecting feedback is a routine practice are still in the minority' (p. 358). Perhaps social work programmes can lead practice development by modelling service user and carer involvement.

Evaluating the overall experience of involvement

We will conclude by drawing out our learning from working with the CU Group and Network. Overall it has worked relatively well as a system of achieving influence over the education of social workers at a local level. In the first year after the network scheme was launched, 6 staff members had engaged with the system, 3 had partially engaged and 2 had not started, from a group of 11 people. A number of significant changes have occurred, perhaps as a result of this process. There is increasing input to teaching by service users and carers across the department. In the previous academic year (2004) they were involved in 23 presentations, compared to 56 in 2005. The process takes time, but we are making progress.

The influence of the CU Group on the University of Dundee's Department of Social Work over the past three years is clear. This has been supported by the research and evaluation that formed part of the SIESWE project. It has moved the social work programme from the inertia outlined in the audit of service user and carer involvement three years ago (Ager and Gee, 2004) to strong involvement with a positive impact (Ager, 2004;

Gee, 2005). However, careful preparation is needed and service users can at times be over-positive in their feedback. Students and teachers alike need to develop understanding and skills in making use of the expertise of service users and carers (Gee, 2005).

The CU Group has worked to contribute to the selection of social work students. As indicated earlier, a representative of the group attends the Programme Committee, and indeed the Programme Committee is chaired by a service user (see Chapter 5). One of the modules in the new MSc in Social Work degree, 'Making Sense of the Caring Experience', originated in the CU Group and has established closer partnership working with organisations and individuals in the locality. This all helps to influence our programme. However, service user and carer involvement is a process, not an event, and will take time to develop fully. What remains a constant is the commitment to the process of change given by service users and carers who support this engagement system and the lecturers who participate in it.

New ways of learning attempt to blur academic boundaries such that service user and carer knowledge and expertise carry more weight. In the learning process it looks like there is a repositioning of carers and service users as teachers. However, structures remain such that academic assessment is made on the basis of institutional judgements outside the influence at this stage of service users and carers. More work is needed to embed and sustain partnerships, such that learning is achieved on a more equitable footing.

Having a voice and influence at the Scottish national level: Scottish Voices

We examine service user and carer influence at a Scotland-wide level through the project's work to develop a national service user and carer group, where parallels are made between national and local university experience in both the drivers and the inhibitors of the progress of involvement. These will be summarised at the end of the chapter. The development of a national service user and carer group began as a task of the SIESWE project. The aim was:

> To establish a series of networks of informed and committed service users and family carers who will serve as informants for the developmental processes underpinning social work education and specifically the assessment process. (SIESWE, 2003)

We drew on the experience and grassroots network base of the User and Carer Group at the University of Dundee and the Service User Panel at the Open University. A key focus was the creation of a forum to strengthen the position – and political voice – of service users and carers involved with social work programmes, to identify and develop best practice, and to influence social work education policy and practice on a larger strategic scale at national level. It was expected in our remit that this could be set up in a matter of months. However, the project management group soon perceived that this could not be a short process:

> It takes time to outreach to individual service users and groups in order to invite them to become involved, and to support their involvement effectively. Sadd (2004, p. 12)

We were unconvinced by the 'cherry-picking' approach, a type of involvement identified as 'placation' by Arnstein (1969), where service users and carers who might be more amenable and uncritical of the organisational context are invited to sit on high-powered committees. We renegotiated our project remit to enable us to begin by operating on a consultative basis, drawing on the experience and views of the service user and carer groups working across the universities in Scotland, to avoid the pitfalls of co-option and containment. An early question concerned the issue of separate groups for service users and carers, as discussed in Chapter 1. We wanted to recognise the different approaches taken by service users and carers involved across Scottish social work programmes, where some programmes opted to organise on the basis of separate groups for carers and service users, and to acknowledge the difference and complexity in needs and care relationships. This is an on-going negotiation.

Early developments towards a Scottish national group

Despite a strongly held commitment to democratic consultation in establishing a national network, we were acutely aware of the limitations of the parameters of the project, inevitably constrained by a timetable and performance criteria set by others. We began to consult through focus groups of service users and carers, and two service user and carer conferences in Glasgow and Perth, to establish interest and direction to the work. Volunteers recruited from the conference participants undertook a further online and postal consultation activity, and a report on the findings was produced (McPhail, 2005). Finally there was a consultation workshop in Perth in order to agree a constitution for the national network, which became known as Scottish Voices. The products of our work, the *Scottish Voices* joint conference report (Ager, 2004) and the report on the consultation process towards a national group (McPhail, 2005), demonstrate our commitment to a grassroots participatory approach.

Partnership practice in the development of a national network

For the Scottish project, the experience of involvement in developing the national network of service users and carers has been challenging. As a project group we experienced at first hand the impact of differing interpretations of partnership and policy: the consumerist/managerial approach and the democratic approach (Beresford and Croft, 2003). The democratic principles to which the project team aspired jarred at times with what appeared to be consumerist/managerial approaches in the wider funding organisation. We considered the views espoused by Braye (2000) of the potential co-operation between people with very different perspectives in this arena. However, some difficulties occurred over editorial control of written material emerging from the project, presentations of material at conferences and ultimately control of the facilitation of the national group. We learnt that promotion of service user and carer control of agendas can be misconstrued as power-seeking behaviour and that vigilance is needed to ensure that service users and carers are not used as political pawns to meet differing agency agendas.

Partnership working needs to take account of important elements such as training, collective support and access, in staff selection; quality assurance measures; monitoring and evaluation; the ethics of user involvement and recognition and resource implications (Beresford and Croft, 2003). In managing the project and in developing a national group we found this framework to be a useful guide. Feedback from the national conferences suggests that the project was relatively successful in meeting these criteria (Ager, 2004).

Networking is vital to address the power imbalance between service users and professional organisations. Our experience is echoed by Branfield *et al.* (2006), who identify a range of barriers to effective networking at a national level, such as transport, issues of accessibility for people in rural areas, and the fragile nature of some service user-led organisations. In Scotland, at a national level attempts were made to address this by rotating meetings across the country. This was only partially successful. There are often logistical and transport issues, which presented considerable barriers for people in some areas. Strong views were expressed by service users and carers not to assume that everyone has access to online facilities. Future communication strategies now include a mix of online, face-to-face and postal methods.

Where there was some limited success in reflecting geographical, social and cultural diversity in the two initial conferences, this was less evident in the composition of a working group to establish the national network. It is a positive indication that some progress is being made in reflecting diversity at a local level, but further proactive and creative solutions are required at a national level. The limited involvement of Black and Minority Ethnic groups and other groups of service users with significant access requirements is highlighted elsewhere (Begum, 2006; Branfield *et al.*, 2006). This remains a high strategic priority for action. The national network project had taken a different direction than the one initially conceptualised, directly as a result of the consultative approach. The focus had broadened and the need for additional funding for a continued period of development had been established. Hosted by SIESWE, Scottish Voices is now a constituted group, chaired by John Dow.

This section charts the early work in setting up a Scottish national group, which laid down the democratic foundations of Scottish Voices and ensured that it was not designed by political or academic strategists but by service users and carers themselves. The essentially political nature of this work may have led to SIESWE later choosing to take a much more directive role than they did in other projects. Institute staff proposed and presented papers in this area and supported development work alongside Mo McPhail and Wendy Ager. These developments were granted additional funding allocated by SIESWE, and this was followed by greater 'hands-on' involvement of SIESWE staff. When the project, 'The Involvement of Users and Carers', ended in 2005 so did the involvement of members of the project management group, save John Dow.

Conclusions

We have examined in some detail service user and carer involvement in social work education at university and national level. We have considered the development of systems of engagement and influence at the University of Dundee and the emergence from this of new models of learning for students that draw on a strong service user and carer perspective. We have then considered how university groups can combine at Scotland-wide level to create a stronger political voice. In this final section our learning from these initiatives will be outlined by considering the factors that promote involvement and the factors that hinder this process.

Factors that promote involvement of service users and carers in social work education

We have found that a *flexible* approach promotes involvement. The CU Group and Scottish Voices operate informally within a formal university or governmental hierarchy: they are groups that are answerable to higher-level groups. Contact is made with each other outside meetings through the internet, web and telephone. The groups have a genuine although tenuous role within the structures of social work education because they carry out functions required through social work education regulations and because they use the structures of the hierarchies within which they operate to put forward ideas. Yet within their formal structures there remain informal networks, fitting processes to suit members. Members have set up and agreed the timing and membership of meetings and environments to suit those who attend. They try to get through required business within time limits in agreed ways – plain systems, plain language and good supports towards inclusion are required.

A second factor that has promoted involvement has been agreeing a *shared purpose and value base*. Members in both groups have ideals about participation that have driven their involvement, and these are outlined in guiding principles. This was a way of overcoming power imbalances and a way of members defining the ethos of the group from the start. The agreed principles have much in common with those of other service user groups (Croft and Beresford, 1993; Turner *et al.*, 2002). These principles have set out a common purpose within the CU Group at Dundee and underpinned the early work towards developing a Scottish network.

A third clear factor in promoting carer and service user involvement is the presence of *funding*. It is essential to achieve funding for the travel expenses of service users and carers as well as remuneration for them for the time that they give to meetings, teaching and allied work. We found that where extra funding was given towards developing a national group this came with conditions with respect to the way we would take forward work. SIESWE has negotiated funding for the initial operation of Scottish Voices following the work carried out at its inception, but it too relies on the contribution of universities, and this is not guaranteed by all but subject to the annual funding constraints of institutions.

A fourth factor that we have found aids participation is the use of *grass-roots networks* to inform and support service users and carers at a local and a national level and to give a wider base to their voice in individual teaching contributions, at meetings within institutions and at Scottish national level. The access of members of management committees to grassroots views of service users and carers across the country ensures that ways of developing networks are soundly based. Similarly the access of academics to service user groups on a regular basis ensures that teaching is well informed. Service user and carer experts by experience cannot claim to be democratically elected representatives, but where they are linked to wider service user and carer groups they speak with a collective voice.

Factors that constrain involvement of service users and carers in social work education

We now consider what does *not* help spread service user and carer influence. A movement towards greater involvement of service users and carers raises 'challenges to professional modes of thinking and operating, emerging as a result of participation' (Carr, 2004, p. v). Behind the rhetoric of shared views, Carr also perceives a lack of organisational responsiveness, commenting that 'a fundamental political commitment to change should be driving participation initiatives' (p. vi). There is a divergence between the rhetoric of participation and inclusiveness and the practice of social workers and social work academics that should be considered (Tyler, 2006). In all the following constraints we can see the exercise of power in direct and indirect ways.

There are some clearly practical issues. In universities these include the pressures of existing workloads for lecturers; the need for more preparation for the lecturers themselves in making use of contact; and for better administration and information for the network as a whole. Within governmental agencies there is the need to be driven by positive images so as to achieve funding and electoral success. Hidden underneath this, amongst students, service users and carers, lecturers and politicians, is the obvious fact that some people are not genuinely committed to a participative way of working within social work, but know enough to keep their opinions to themselves. However, much research in this area points out that being prepared to share expertise with those one works for is a process that will take time to take hold, but that given that time, views and practices can change (Carr, 2004; Tew et al., 2006).

A second constraint lies in funding. Firstly there is a lack of ring-fenced funding for service user and carer involvement in universities and at national level, and secondly there is complexity of administration within the benefits system. Significant difficulties arise not only from the amount of money people are allowed to earn without a negative impact on welfare benefits, but also from the complexity of information about what does and does not count. The Shaping Our Lives team recommended changes to benefit arrangements to clarify payments for involvement work (Turner and Beresford, 2005 p. v). A Department of Health report (Cooley and Lawrence 2006), seeks to clarify the situation regarding fair and appropriate rewards but has not made recommendations to raise the amount of money people are allowed to receive before their benefits are affected. At a national level secure and sustained funding is a baseline condition for such groups to thrive, with funding arrangements which do not compromise the independence and integrity of service user and carer representatives.

Following from this point is a third constraint to service user and carer involvement. This is that the independent and flexible nature of service user and carer influence sits uneasily at times with the formal hierarchies that are universities and national government. This has parallels to service user and carer work in other institutions. An examination of service user-led research within a health board, for example, concluded that barriers to involvement arose from the often inflexible and bureaucratic nature of hospitals, where roles and uniforms allow access and the lack of these amongst service user group researchers posed difficulties (Allam et al., 2004). Large university and governmental systems do not at times meet the needs entailed in involving service users and carers. Even within a hierarchical organisation, line-managed responsibilities are not always clear. Similarly, university financial and audit systems cannot take on board methods of token payment to service users and carers.

A fourth constraint to involvement lies in the fact that, whilst informality is central to network relationships and the CU Group, it can inhibit efficient and egalitarian practice too. Membership of groups in the community can change and new members have little understanding of the network process, effectively disempowering them. Links that do not have the reinforcement of well financed organisation can disappear over time. Contacts between CU members and network members can be ragged and therefore supports or controls are weak. Even within CU meetings informality may not guarantee an equal voice. Members of the CU Group can be ignored in favour of the more articulate members. Similar experiences occurred at the national level.

A fifth constraint lies in the language that is valued in an academic or governmental environment: the language of documentation, formal meetings and academic papers. Service users and carers at meetings within institutions call to order those using unfamiliar terms and highlight the principle of plain English. This cannot extend so easily beyond meetings. How far can service users and carers have genuine influence when documentation and the spoken word of institutions can be a barrier to the entry of others?

Summary

In distilling lessons from our experience of working with service users and carers in social work education we have suggested the following to characterise good practice, more fully laid out in Good Practice Guidelines (Ager et al., 2006):

- There are systems in place to ensure all those involved in social work education whether as teachers or in administration have access to the views of service users and carers.

- Principles for good working are debated and agreed by service user and carer groups and followed by the institutions that use and support such groups.

- Power differentials located in individuals and institutions are acknowledged and efforts made to redress imbalances.

- Informal and flexible systems are promoted to create a comfortable environment for service users and carers.

- There are adequate supports and training for all involved but especially service users and carers.

- There is adequate funding to cover the time and expenses of all service users and carers involved in the system.

- Priority time is allocated to lecturers and others involved with social work education to engage with service users and carers.

- There is a formal requirement to work together alongside the process of engaging hearts and minds of both service users/carers and university staff.

- There are transparent systems to monitor and review progress of service user and carer involvement.

- Service users and carers groups are set up and based on the views of service users and carers themselves and not shaped by more powerful interests.

- Key academics or professionals involved in the development of service user and carer groups need to have a conviction about the importance of participatory approaches to social work so as to help ensure this is maintained in less participatory political and academic systems.

CHAPTER 4

Expert Knowledge: A Carer's Perspective

Norma McSloy

Introduction: becoming a representative of carers

In this chapter I will examine the events that led to my becoming a represent-ative of carers with Enable in Scotland and within the local authority who provide care for my son, and later with the University of Dundee CU and with the SIESWE Project 3.3 Group. I shall also consider what has helped and what has not helped in my work to influence the way that social workers practice and are trained. I did not choose this path, it was chosen for me, and there are many parts of it that other carers will recognize. I became a member of the CU Group at the University of Dundee and then with the SIESWE Project because I knew what a pivotal role social workers had in my son's life. If change was to happen it should begin with their professional educa-tion by the inclusion of teaching from service users and carers.

My experiences as a carer and what they have taught me

My career as a carer started with the birth of my son Ewan. My son, Ewan, is 32 years old. When he describes himself he says he is a shepherd who looks after pet sheep. Ewan has a learning disability, is on the autistic spectrum and has obsessive compulsive disorder. Although he sees himself as an adult with the same rights as everyone else, he realises that he does need support and he knows that I am his Welfare Guardian. My life has taken a different course because Ewan has a learning disability. There have been significant events throughout my son's life when decisions have been made which seem to have largely been determined by what resources were available or what was politically correct at that time. By contrast, the motivating force in my involvement has been to find the best outcome for my son, and this has led me to develop skills to fight for rights in all sorts of areas such as health, education and social services.

We noticed that Ewan did not mix with other children and was not making progress as he should, and when he started nursery for two days a week the staff were quite concerned with him in comparison to his peers. When he was about to start school a year later, the nursery notified the school to say he was having problems. This was quite a shock, as they did not let us know they had taken this action. My point here is that as carers we were not always in the know and we were not always listened to. The message was clear; if we wanted something for Ewan we had to campaign for it ourselves.

We sought a diagnosis for Ewan's difficulties. We felt that the professionals did not seem aware of the significance of a diagnosis for parents, such that we could understand what we were dealing with. As a result we were not able to grieve for the son that we had hoped to bring up or come to terms with the kind of difficulties our son would face. It was years later that I recognised the volume of emotional and physical stress that had been internalised during this period. In the early stages we got no positive feedback at all – it was always 'difficulty with speech', 'difficulty with movement', 'difficulty with language', 'difficulty with social interaction'. This was extremely depressing. We had a job to do and yet we felt these comments had a very negative effect on us all as a family. It felt as if there was something we were not doing right and that was why Ewan behaved that way. My husband used to say to me before going into a case conference or review: 'It is not your fault nor is it mine or Ewan's. We just have to do the best we can for him.' As carers we felt that professionals are often unaware of the anxieties and stresses we carry, added to by the ignorance of others. These points of view must be conveyed to student professionals.

As parents we have been consistently involved with Ewan in seeking out the best provision possible, from the early days in trying to ensure full-time primary education to recent times in getting his own tenancy. When Ewan was five, my husband Joe wrote to the education department:

> I am writing regarding the future education of my son, Ewan ... he is currently attending infants school but only in the mornings. The headmistress feels that the school cannot cope with our son full time without the provision of auxiliary help and I understand that that help is still required next term. My wife also understands from the headmistress that due to Government cuts, the school will have difficulty providing the additional help required ... I must let you know that in the opinion of my wife and me, we think it is essential that our son receive full-time education as of next term. It is also our view that he is happy at the school and will learn there and it would have a very serious adverse effect if he were not allowed to continue his education there...

As parents we learnt the language and approach of professionals and I appreciate how hard it is for many service users and carers to understand and work with the language of the local authority. In one report from a case conference his teacher wrote:

Ewan is an individual, never disobedient, unkind or rough. He is generally cheerful and loving. He quickly earns the affection of people he meets and the other children accept him and encourage him.

I can still remember how these remarks were like a balm to a very raw wound. My learning, as a carer prepared to campaign for better services and for service users and carers, is that professionals must always try to work from positives about those they work with. This can help and encourage us and needs to be a skill that students develop.

When Ewan was eight years old we once again tried to influence the services provided for our son. My husband again initiated contact with the education department, to ensure good education provision. Following carefully worded recommendations my husband added:

I think that it is vitally important that parents know how professionals see Ewan and equally important that the parents share with the professionals how they see him.

During his school years, we tried to integrate Ewan into community activities, although he was not always welcomed with open arms. He was refused entry to one scout group because 'he would hold the other kids back'. However, he eventually joined a scout group and did other activities including Riding for the Disabled, youth clubs and the Duke of Edinburgh Award. My husband became a parent governor of Ewan's new special school in Scotland. I was treasurer of a committee raising funds for a mini-bus, so my social life at this time included helping to organise ceilidhs, fashion shows, Christmas fairs etc. Our view was that these activities needed support to keep going and *crucially for us* we needed the social interaction for our son. Professionals in training need to understand the vital importance of integration into normal activities and the need for this to be supported by the strategies of those who make decisions in communities.

Another milestone much later was our son's Future Needs Meeting, which was attended by many people who did not contribute one word to the proceedings. I remember my husband remarked to me at the time that the school dinner lady knew our son better than most of them. They recommended a college place for Ewan, which ended up as the wrong decision, and at this time my husband died. I now had to undertake a central role as a carer. I became Ewan's Welfare Guardian; I attended all meetings. A few years later Ewan began to suffer from great anxieties. It was the hardest two years of my life. He would not be left alone and lost all his independence and confidence which had been so hard to build up. He had obsessive compulsive disorder. This led to his being compulsorily admitted to hospital and led to me undertaking a course in cognitive therapy to understand how to work with this condition. They said this was as good as it was going to get, but I could not accept it and pushed for something to be done. I did not believe that professionals' views on everything would be considered to have more value than mine or my family's.

My learning as a carer working with professionals

Before we meet, professionals have a position of power with service users and carers. At case conferences they set the agenda – if there are issues they do not want to deal with they exclude them. You are often not given all the information to make good choices. They have discussed our situation beforehand so that possibilities are eliminated already, our power has already gone. Even where you wish to object, push or go to MPs the information about how to do this is not there. Service users and carers have strength through our knowledge of the individual concerned. If professionals listen to us I think that fewer mistakes will be made. Honesty and openness is important: if people 'tell it to us like it is' we can work with this and can make our own decisions as to what to do. It is disheartening when people come to meetings with completely different agendas – where Ewan and his needs are not at the centre, but things such as sticking to budget. Who checks on the workers and managers when they have a long history of work with you and may have their biases? Failure to check and to challenge was at the root of problems discussed in the Borders Inquiry into deficiencies in the care and treatment of a woman with learning disabilities.

My experience as a carer consultant and what that has taught me

Ewan living in his own home with support coincided with me being more actively involved in what was happening in Scotland in the fields of health, social work and social work education. I remember being invited to join our local planning group to implement *The Same as You* (Scottish Executive, 2000). I did not feel very confident and was rather overwhelmed by the professionals there. However, they were offering us an opportunity to have our say, and I for one could not let that pass me by. Heart pounding and voice shaking, I stood up and gave my opinion. I subsequently went along to lots of meetings on a wide range of subjects including respite, profound needs, employment, day opportunities, leisure time, health etc.

I observed and learned a lot in the way that our local authority took *The Same as You* forward. Looking back, it was a one-way process, with very little account taken of us. We joined the planning group with very little information either about the planning process itself, or about implementation or the financial provisions made. It was in their gift what they told us, and in their gift to use or not use the views we expressed. We had no means of knowing what was being reported. However, I attended as many meetings and subgroups as I possibly could to make sure at least one carer or service user was sitting at the table. There were some professionals who were not happy working with the same few carers and service users who came forward time after time. I have to say there were a few professionals who were involved for a very long time within the learning disability team that we were not thrilled about either, but we had to deal with them whatever our views were. Most carers did not have the time and some simply did not get involved because they had heard it all before and nothing had changed – or should I say, changed to what they wanted for the person they cared for.

In this process I have had the opportunity to learn about all manner of service planning and provision. I could see that the power did not shift and the money has stayed with those in power. Although Partnership in Practice plans were submitted to the Scottish Executive, not all that was included in those documents was carried out. We have not had another planning meeting since the Partners in Practice documents went to the Scottish Executive. Was it all a waste of time and energy? Any involvement that does not value the use of people's time and wastes that time by not using the outcomes to influence change should be questioned.

During this time, I became increasingly busy on other fronts too. I was asked if I would become a director of a local voluntary organisation promoting inclusion for people with a learning disability. I also became an elected member of the Scottish Council of Enable Scotland. I was asked to represent learning disabilities on the Carers Strategy Committee. I attended a truly inspirational conference in Edinburgh called 'The Future is Purple'. This was the first of many events ranging from social work reviews and health service information-gathering days to workshops with service users and carers talking about what their needs were. I did person-centred training and advocacy training, enabling me to advocate for service users or carers. I benefited from several days' training delivered by a lawyer on the Adults with Incapacity (Scotland) Act (2000). I did awareness training on vulnerable adults, committee chairing training and community regeneration training. I completed a ten-day course, 'Re-thinking the Future', delivered by Common Knowledge in Glasgow. I also took time to undertake equal opportunity training and was able to sit on many interviewing panels.

My experiences of involvement at the University of Dundee

My initial contact with the University of Dundee was just before I joined the CU Group (the Service User and Carer Group): it was a conference on the subject of the new undergraduate social work degree at Dundee. I know a few service users and carers were invited along, but it was very much a day for those involved in social work education. I left early, as did all the other carers and service users. I can only speak for myself when I say I knew this was not an occasion when I felt comfortable putting across my point of view. A very important point to note about such initial encounters – the service users and carers might all have decided never to come back. Fortunately they did. In the second meeting we had, I felt that concerns voiced had been taken on board. The academics running the meeting made us very much part of the day; they made an effort to include us in at every stage. You realised that they needed you to develop the new degrees and you wanted to be able to influence the teaching. However, even in this more positive meeting I thought that on the day the lack of information on what was being discussed prevented me from making a full contribution. To me this shows that slowly and over time the ideas of professionals and academics can change if service users and carers can get their views taken on board.

Through my work in the CU Group I was asked to contribute to training about community care, learning disabilities and being a carer. Not for the first time I had qualms getting up to speak, but I saw it as important that students heard at first hand about the networks of people who use services and their carers. Because the students asked good questions at the end I think that they were taking my experiences and views on board well, and I received positive feedback from them too.

The CU Group were and are now major contributors to teaching about community care. We were also involved in preparation for practice, when we offered our advice on how students could get feedback from clients. There were quite a few sessions with students using role-play and videos to develop their skills for their future roles as social workers. I remember remarking to the lecturer at the time that during the many interviews my son and I had with social workers I had not thought for one minute they had advance training in interviews or ordinary communication skills. I said that my son and I of course had no advance training so I wondered if we were disadvantaged and if by empowering the social worker you disempowered people like us. The lecturer had never thought of it in that way before and agreed it was sometimes a good thing to hear my thoughts on that. I have helped in the development of teaching programmes and even suggested an idea for one of the modules, The Caring Experience (described in Chapter 5). The module was based on my belief that students need to see what it is like to live my life for 24 hours. I begin to see that some of the learning from my years as a carer is being put to good use as I help to educate new social workers.

My learning as a carer contributing to teaching

When I teach students the student social workers do not have Ewan my son in common with me. I cannot always give my view honestly to social workers in practice because he needs services – I am dependent on them. In class I am free of this. The attitude of academics helps: you would like them to respect your contribution, value it! This makes you confident in delivery. We need good briefing about what the students need to know or want to know, the level they are at. We need briefing about the background to their learning and a clear focus about what we should cover. We have to be accepted for the people we are. We should not be expected to be the same as university lecturers. What we do is share our personal situations and our experiences in order that students will be able to work in a different way. It is vital that service users and carers always work in ways that they are totally comfortable with.

The role of the carer does not always prepare you for teaching – if you have not had the benefit of a university education. However, it is more important for you to be confident in yourself to start with than to be academic. A patronising attitude does not help and this passes on to the student. On the first occasion when I taught a class about the carer's perspective in community care I felt the power of what I was doing come to me in quite an unexpected way. At last I had an opportunity to influence future social workers – there were no two ways about it. The academic trusted me and knew I was an experienced carer and campaigner and would be even-handed in my approach.

The CU Group at the University of Dundee

I have been a member of the CU Group at the University of Dundee for a number of years. The group meets every month and is involved in giving guidance and support to all aspects of selection, teaching and assessment. We sit on the governing body, the Programme Committee. Being a member of the group has given all of us who take part the opportunity to use our experience of social workers to influence social work education. All our members are usually part of a group or network. Hearing and recording the voices of these networks will hopefully guarantee a wider participation, although we will always have to make sure our efforts include people who may be harder to reach. When you know university lecturers and students are committed to the involvement of people who use services and their carers and are not just 'ticking the box', it has a different feel to it and everyone responds accordingly. You have to prioritise honesty, openness, commitment, equality and inclusion to involve service users and carers in social work education. As a CU member reported in the evaluation done of the group:

> I would not have stayed a member of this group had it just been 'tokenistic'. Our contribution was recorded in minutes. Our influence on the use of the type of language, the style of meetings, our statement of intent, our contributions to the two conferences, our talks to students were wholly our words and opinions – uncensored – I believe the university staff wanted and needed our contributions. I felt they were valuable to professionals and we also were able to appreciate the contribution university staff made to the process – it was very much a two-way learning process (Ferguson, 2005).

*Learning from involvement in the CU Group at
the University of Dundee*

It appears to me that service users and carers as well as academics get something from the CU Group. It is a two-way process: we are all learning from it and there is satisfaction in this. For example, when I met with others about selection processes there was a genuine exchange of information; I felt we had had an influence there and in lots of other ways.

There are not really power issues present – some members are more confident than others but that does not make for issues. What helps us work together are a number of things. Having good administration back-up from Wendy and now Agnes, getting papers in advance, getting payment for attending which puts a value on our time. Knowing that we come from different disciplines, but that they give a balanced viewpoint and understanding, a comradeship. The individuals involved are nice, and respect is present. What does not help is the times when there is a lack of clear information at the start. We need enough information to contribute and to influence, but not too much.

As carer consultant with the SIESWE project

I applied and was successful in becoming a carer consultant on the Scottish project, Project 3.3, because of my experience in working with the CU Group at Dundee. It was from the research gathered from this project that John Dow, the service user consultant, and I, together with Mo McPhail, Wendy Ager and others, formed the steering group for a National Group of Influence to draw together representation from service users and carers linked to the nine universities in Scotland offering social work education. This enabled a more robust and even knowledge exchange across Scotland between all those involved in the teaching of social work and social care. John Dow and I co-chaired this group and we were very determined to make a valued and unique contribution to social work education. At the beginning of work with the national group we had researched the views of service users and carers as part of the project. This gathering of views had led to the two Scottish Voices national conferences, where we got a mandate about how to go forward. At this stage it was very much about listening to service users and carers and building up a national group from grassroots.

For me everything changed at the next stage when the steering group was set up. When we all came together to meet with the Institute it was apparent that some people were more powerful than others. The balance of power had changed. The Institute provided further funding for the group so had to have a presence, but I felt that, like us, they had their own objectives. It is perhaps fair, but it meant that the group would be trying to meet Institute aims as well as those of service users and carers. The little stream that we were as individual service users and carers was being washed away by a bigger stream.

We lost our direct connection between ourselves and the universities. If you give your time but are not getting anything from it you question whether the outcome and influence justify the time spent.

Summary

My life as Ewan's carer has taught me lessons that I now take into my work as a representative of carers. In short these are:

- Service users and carers have great knowledge about their needs and the needs of those they care for, and professionals need to learn the skill of listening to them.

- Parents and carers can be a great resource if they are brought into discussions and decisions. Parents and carers often feel very power-less amongst the experts when they seek the best for their family. Professionals should be aware of this and seek to make them less powerless.

- Professional workers need to step into the shoes of carers and understand what it is like in their daily lives, and this goes for students too.

- Above all we do not wish to be used in a tokenistic way. Service users and carers and professionals need to think about this together when they set up joint working.

- Formal language and meetings are not helpful to all service users and carers; it must be remembered that the university environment can be intimidating for many.

- We need to see change from our involvement. When we think students may genuinely learn new points of view or teaching programmes are altered because of our contributions it seems worthwhile.

- Some professionals seem to have the skills and manner that encourage you to work with them and others do not. These skills must be part of teaching to social work students.

- At times it is necessary for service users and carers to challenge and be heard. This challenge may be difficult for the academics or social workers at the receiving end, but at the end of the day they hold great power over us when they make decisions and it seems fair that just occasionally they experience these frustrations.

CHAPTER 5

Our Journey:
Perspectives from People who Use Services

John Dow

Introduction

I am a service user. What then is the difference between you and me? After all we all use various services of one kind or another. Most of us use building societies, banks, shops, garages, doctors, dentists etc. So why is my state-ment about being a service user different? Well, some of us are different: we have to use services, not always through choice, but often through a recognised need. In my own personal circumstances, I need the support of professional service providers such as health services, social work services, but unlike others I do not have the same right of choice. I cannot look around for a better return for my custom; I am not able to change these things as, for example, I may be able to change my type of transport as my aspirations for a better and faster car change.

However, I can through my involvement in the design and delivery of services help the professional service provider to identify the needs of people like me. Why can I achieve this? Because I am a *service specialist.* The pro-fessional service provider may, or indeed may not, have all the qualities and skills they feel are required to deliver the right service in the right areas to the right people. However, they need people like me, not just me, or a few people like me, but many people like me. We are the service specialists, we know what services we require, and our carers know the support they and we need to meet our care needs. None of us is able to guarantee that our views are fully reflective of all service users or carers. We must build strong networks across the country to make sure the views of those who require services are as fully represented as we (that includes professionals, carers and users) can possibly make them, especially of those groups or individuals who may be difficult to reach or engage with. If we grasp this opportunity for full, honest, transparent, valued input from every stakeholder, we may begin to see real change. We may see involvement leading to real and valuable influence.

Now this view is not new. It's not a wonderful clever answer to the problem of designing services. It is, rather, common sense. I don't go to my local paper shop, pay for my papers and ask, 'Can you check my gearbox and clutch, as I've got to drive a hundred miles?' I rely on the professionals who know about my car and they rely on me as the driver of the car to let them know what I feel may be wrong. We work together. In the same way, we can all work together to design the services that people need, not only now, but in the future.

Before we can achieve this balance between professional and user perspectives, however, we need to look at some basic questions. Why should service users be involved? How do we (service users) know we've made a difference? What, if anything, has changed? Do we (service users) need to be 'different' when we are dealing with the various 'powers that be' in health and social services? What's in it for us if we stay involved? Do we have real power? Do they have the power? What *is* real power? These are interesting and thought-provoking questions. Within this chapter I will bring my personal experiences, and those of other service users, of the journey we have been on. This is a journey which for many of us seems like a road that never ends; a road that has many twists and turns. It is a journey that for some of us has become too tiring, too long without any sign of real change. It is a journey where our need for support to sustain us has often gone unrecognised.

Starting point

So where did our journey begin? In my experience there has been an enthusiasm for the input and involvement of service users and our carers in the design and delivery of services for at least twenty years. Over that period health boards, local authorities, GPs and all professionals tasked by the politicians to deliver services fit for purpose have sought our views. However, many of them appear only interested in, as one TV programme puts it, 'who wants to be a millionaire?' Where statutory bodies could demonstrate that they were actively involving and 'hearing' the views of users and carers, they would in return receive 'loadsamoney' from the Scottish Executive or other funding streams, because they had heard our views.

They went around and asked individuals if they wanted to be involved. They were then able to state in their business plans that they were committed to the new ideal of user and carer involvement, of everyone being equal partners, and in return their political masters looked more favourably on their future budget plans. So initially everyone was happy. We felt involved and they had assured us that we were 'equal partners'. I was allowed to sit at the big table. I was given expenses (although in some instances I had to ask) to cover my travel costs to the venues, initially at 25 pence per mile. At this time, this seemed to be real change, something new and exciting. It was good to have our views and concerns 'heard'. But what happened after we had been 'heard'? Well, we were invited to other meetings; we were paid more expenses; we had more sandwiches and biscuits; we went to more meetings and we received more expenses, and our views were heard again. For a time this seemed to meet the needs of those involved within the process of user and carer involvement and, as they say, everything in the garden was rosy. We had been 'heard'. They, the 'professionals,' had engaged with and 'heard' our views, so we got our expenses and coffee; they got extra money for their budgets. Our journey had been good. We had been 'heard.' But was this enough?

We were beginning to see that as our journey progressed, our fellow travellers were changing. Some had left the car, and others had joined in our journey. We were beginning to ask, as our expectations changed, what is in this for me – and others like me – who believe in the need for real involvement that would lead to real influence? How would they, the professionals, our partners, demonstrate that our views and knowledge were valued? Were we still a key part of the journey, and had our work led to real change in the way services were being delivered? In Fife, Scotland, for example, in 2001 all residents and members of NHS staff were given the opportunity to shape the future look of health services following the launch of a consultation document called 'Right for Fife'. Interestingly this strategy has been now renamed 'The Health Agenda', and we are told no one should refer to the old 'Right for Fife'. Somehow no one felt it was important to tell those people who use services of this change. I suppose it's just a name, or could it be an indication of something more worrying? I'll return to this later when I mention communication.

Many of us who had been involved in the user and carer movement wanted to believe that this Fife initiative was going to be different. This new and exciting opportunity would enable us to be recognised as partners, trusted and welcomed to the process of designing services to meet our needs. Our views and concerns about what was good and bad in the services we received would be welcomed. They, the professionals, said we 'WOULD BE HEARD'. In exchange for being heard, we should and could trust them, the professionals, that the same never-ending journey would begin to show real change. 'We are not in this to repeat the same mistakes made over the last ten or twelve or perhaps more years' (statement from a manager of mental health services in Fife). This was going to be different because they had said so; after all, we were being invited to the process as *equal partners*. We would receive our travel expenses; we would get some more sandwiches and biscuits. And above all, they kept telling us, we would be heard. This had to be good, didn't it? They could be trusted, couldn't they? We were equal partners, sharing power, weren't we?

Sharing the journey

Before I give my own reflections on these issues, I'd like to share a few of the views of others who have shared this long journey with me. As service specialists, experts by experience, carers, service users, whatever we choose to be called, we can act, we have the ability to do, and we are able to INFLU-ENCE, if everyone accepts we are different. We have different needs and may require different supports. Each of us, whether we are users or carers, we each bring different experiences, qualities, knowledge and skills. We are not EQUAL, and my label may not be as big or important as yours. But our views are valuable; they are necessary and are based on real experiences, real hurt and sometimes, real anger.

I asked some of my friends and those who had been part of the user and carer movement for real change what they felt about the process, and the levels of power within the process. Here are some of their views:

> They seem to need their LABELS to make me feel inferior, or to stop me being part of the debate. We've said for years that we don't need labels. None of us is better or worse than each other. We just work and support each other. Why can't they see this – is it a power thing? (Lynne [not her real name])

> They use their labels to show their power. They think the label is POWER, power for power's sake. (Brenda [not her real name])

> For me the label doesn't matter but the sandwiches need to be good. (Andy)

I suppose that if we look at Andy's comment, we have a good chance of success if we make sure the sandwiches are good. But knowing him as I do, I think this is his way of saying he no longer believes we are achieving much, if anything, at all. He often says after a meeting, or after I've asked him to support me at meetings, 'I don't mind coming along but am I making any real difference, or am I just making up the numbers, to make them [the professionals] look good?' He has also said, 'I will attend, and yes I do want to help, but I don't know if we are changing anything at times.'

Keeping going

How then do we keep our enthusiasm going to achieve real change which will have a positive outcome for service users and carers? I don't believe 'the great and the good' need the same type of support as me or people like me. After all, they told us things were going to be different. We could trust them – we were equal partners. They from their position of power, behind their label, don't need to worry about trust. They only need to show to their political and financial masters that they are doing the job within their job description. And, unfortunately, if my experience and those like me is right, that job description doesn't ask them to demonstrate that they know *how* to work alongside us. It doesn't ask them to show how they have given power to us, or to show how we can trust them.

Now before any one thinks I'm either stating the obvious, or taking this opportunity to knock those in power, I am pleased to be able to share with you the outcome of a conversation I had with the Chairman of NHS Fife, when attending a meeting to 'map Fife's Health Plan'. At this meeting when we all stopped for, yes you've guessed it, tea, coffee and biscuits, he asked me how I thought the event was going. Not wanting to appear negative, I said the ideas were good, but that the audience was rather weighted in favour of the professionals, with only a very small 'token' user or carer representation. This in my opinion seemed to reinforce that there were individuals in power who either felt uncomfortable engaging with users and carers, or did not know how to achieve involvement and influence of users and carers. To his credit the Chairman asked if I thought this was an oversight, or did I feel there was a skills or knowledge gap? My reply was to say that I felt it was a skills and knowledge gap. The Chairman then asked if we could meet up at a later date to address the concerns I had raised from my own perspective and those of others in Fife. The meeting has now been arranged, and I am looking forward to it. I feel that on this occasion, a person in power demonstrated that we can work together honestly and transparently to collectively shape change.

Yet it's not always been so positive. I recently attended a meeting with representatives from the health board, the local authority and others. During this meeting, I mentioned that some individuals and groups within Fife were worried that they didn't know who they could speak to if there was a problem within their group. A senior manager asked in a rather vague way, where was I hearing this, as they weren't aware of there being a problem. It was only when I said that this issue had been raised by me over many months that the chairman of the meeting agreed that the issue of communication needed to be addressed, not just for the benefit of service users, but also for members of staff who were finding it difficult to know who was running what, with the various changes of responsibility.

If we can't get basic communication right, how can we trust and begin to move through involvement to achieve real influence? I understand that the issue has been raised again and hope that the chairman will ensure that we see things changing with regard to communication. If not, I can rely on the minutes of the meeting to challenge why the issue hasn't been addressed. At times I do have the confidence that this issue of communication will change – yet why do I feel I'm the thorn in their sides? Why don't I feel comfortable at times when at meetings? Why do I feel I'm valued when they ask me do pieces of work, but not valued when I challenge them? At such times they seem to forget about partnership. When challenge comes, lines of power are drawn again. But change can only be achieved if that power is shared.

This need to demonstrate sharing power and trust is not a new way of working. The need to demonstrate trust was highlighted by Shemmings and Shemmings (1995):

From the research, it seems that two conditions are necessary before those receiving health and welfare services will even think about participation. They need to experience mutuality with those providing services, and they must experience trust. But this 'trust' requires an additional dimension to that originally described by American pioneers and researchers in the field of counselling and psychotherapy in the 60s and 70s. When the power relationship is structurally unequal, for trust to be experienced, and then sustained, it must be demonstrated by professionals at all times. Health and welfare professionals cannot expect clients and patients to have faith in them: they will regularly need to prove themselves to be trustworthy.

So how do we as service users and carers see these issues around mutual trust and power? Are they as important now as they appeared in 1995? The short answer is yes. Indeed, as our journey moves from one of involvement to one of real influence, it is perhaps more important that we see trust. We need trust that shows we are valued; that we are key partners; that we are being listened to, not just heard; that our being listened to and valued has led to and will continue to lead to real influence and change, now and in the future. We need trust that we are sharing the power to bring about change. We have so much to gain by visiting and revisiting this theme whenever we meet as partners. But we have much more to lose if we fail to show that trust in our continued journey together. All of our work and our achievements can be lost in one day, simply by a thoughtless act which fails to reassure us all that we are trusted, valued, respected partners, no matter what badge we wear, or what power we may feel we have.

Achievements on the way

From my own experience and those of other service users and carers involved in this process, there is a feeling that we are in danger of losing some, if not all, of the achievements we have made in the last eight or so years.

We are beginning again to ask each other why should we bother. Are things any different or is it, simply, here we go again? Sometimes it feels that no one really wants us to be a part of their agenda for change. They just want us there, so they can say we were at the table, at the meeting, whatever. So they can tick the boxes.

These are some of the feelings and views of a number of the users and carers I talk to and meet with in various settings and groups. That's why it's important that those professionals we work alongside take responsibility themselves to convince us that things have and are changing. Someone explained to me the 'DATA' syndrome – 'we Do All That Already'. Many of us are beginning to feel that we are in danger of the power brokers beginning to use this response as a way of saying that they, the professionals, the experts, are engaging with service users and carers. We are at the table so why are we complaining? What are they not doing?

Sarah Carr (2004) writes of the inequality of power in the service user and provider relationship:

> Power issues underlie the majority of identified difficulties with effective service user led change. The message is that any service user participation initiative requires continual awareness of the context of power relations in which it is being conducted. (p. 14)

For those of us who have been on this journey, we are now seeing this as one of the main issues, if not the most important issue, that needs to be addressed by the professionals. They need to start to walk the walk, not simply continue to talk the talk. The people who use services and who have been on this journey to influence how those services are designed and delivered see the power differences between them and the professionals, and the unfairness this causes, as being the single most important issue to contend with. As Andy would say, 'the high heid yins need to see what it's like at the coal face.'

Those of us who use services or support those who use services grasped many years ago that we need to share our power in order to support one another. I believe that the destination is not a measure of success. Success is rather being able to continue our journey with all its twists and turns – with support when we need it. I know I can call on the experience of others, draw on their skill and knowledge built up over many years, to continue our journey towards real influence and change. Which leaves me to ask what are they, the professionals, those who feel they hold power, what are they doing to demonstrate they want to be part of our journey with us? For me there have been a number of examples of sharing power. Some have been extremely positive and others not so positive.

Involvement with social work education

I feel that my involvement with the Carer and User Group within the University of Dundee has been, both for the entire group and for us all as individuals within the group, a very positive experience. Since we began to meet as a group, we have shared our experiences and we have moved forward the process of service users and carers being at the centre of social work education. For example, we have worked collectively in the design of both degrees in social work being undertaken by the university. Our strengths and knowledge have been sought by those who manage and deliver the degrees. They, through our group, have seen real benefit from working collectively; we have shared our strengths and knowledge to introduce ideas, such as the module entitled 'Making Sense of the Caring Experience' suggested by our group.

We have seen the need to change the way in which we work, as the membership of the group changes with new members coming on board, bringing their strengths and knowledge. It has meant an opportunity to take time out for some of the more established members, without feeling guilty or that they will no longer be needed. Through this process of change and development we have recognised the need to continually communicate, negotiate and support each other. Each person should have an opportunity to use their skills and experience, sharing the work of the group. Each of us needs to work at our individual pace, to take a break from driving the car to direct the journey or perhaps simply to be a back-seat passenger enjoying the journey. It is important for the professionals who work with us to recognise that there is a danger that, for whatever reason, they may be over-protective of us as users and carers. They, like us, need to celebrate and support our individual and collective development.

Another example of change within this process of involvement and influence occurred when, as a representative of the CU Group, I was asked to be the Chairman for the Programme Committee of the Faculty of Social Work within the University of Dundee. At the time of accepting this offer, I was not aware of any other 'non-academic' being offered this role within any other university. With support from the Head of Faculty and others within the university, I have been able to take on this role and believe this to be a real demonstration of sharing power, valuing what I, as a member of the Carer and User Group, can bring to the table.

For some this may seem that the professionals were merely trying to look good, to be seen as fully engaging in the process of sharing power without much real effort. They could say to their peers, 'Aren't we good? Look, we have appointed a user who is not an academic to the position of Chair of our Programme Committee'. For me and the members of the university Carer and User Group this demonstrated that my skills as a service user member were fully recognised. I do not bring the power of a title such as 'Dr' or 'Professor' or 'Head of Department', but I do bring my skills of managing meetings and I am able to question some of the processes of this important committee. I have, with the support of others within the Programme Committee, introduced small yet effective areas of change. An example of this is the way that the business of the committee is managed. Before I undertook the role of chair, business to do with the students, and with users and carers, took place at the end of the agenda. I asked to change this so that we deal with these items at the beginning of our meeting. This was fully supported by the professionals. I disagree with those who may say that this opportunity to take up the role of chair was merely an exercise in good PR, to gain points with the political masters. I became a member of this committee through membership of the Carer and User Group. My skills and abilities were recognised as a committee member and I was invited to become chair on that basis.

I would like there to be more opportunities for this type of change. Perhaps we now need to look at how we identify the qualities of users and carers. How do we ensure that they know what is expected of them when they undertake this type of work? How do we as users and carers celebrate our skills and knowledge and, more importantly, identify what support or training we may need? Maybe we now need to look at a sort of loose 'job spec' to ensure that the contributions of us all, no matter what our label or job may be, are based on a realistic appraisal of our particular skills and expertise. It is important that users and carers do not feel 'out of our depth', but rather that our skills, qualities, and experiences are recognised and we receive the right kind of support to work together to achieve shared objectives, values, aims and aspirations. We need to know what is expected of us as users or carers and what we can expect from the process.

Influence at a Scotland-wide level

Another example of this was when Norma McSloy and I were asked to be part of the management group to develop a national network of users and carers to influence social work programmes across Scotland. Both Norma and I were aware of the commitment expected by each of us, and we were able to work as real partners in this process. We brought our skills and experience to work alongside Wendy Ager, Iain Ferguson, Maggie Gee and Mo McPhail, who brought their special skills. This was two-way traffic. A national group of users and carers involved in social work education, Scottish Voices, has now been established as a result of this joint work. At one time in working with others there was a perception that we, as users and carers, were the passengers to be driven by and given directions by the professionals. But now we are setting our agendas; the professionals are asking us if we could undertake pieces of work, review reports; our views are actively sought after. We must always be aware that we need to visit and revisit how this happens, to ensure that we are doing the driving and we, whilst working with and respecting the professionals, need to decide the direction of our journey and the speed that we will travel. My experience of being part of these processes has helped me to see possibilities of change and ways of working together to achieve real influence.

Recognising qualities and skills

This has reinforced my belief that I am more than simply my care or service needs. I also have real experiences and knowledge gained from the various jobs undertaken since leaving school. My care needs are important, but they are only part of me. My knowledge and skills have been recognised, and this recognition has allowed me once again to feel valued and respected for being me. This is one of the main reasons we continue to be involved. Through sitting at the same table as 'the great and the good', we gain a degree of personal recovery in our lives. We can gain a feeling of having shared knowledge, and having our views respected, which will lead to change now and in the future.

What can professional people who need to answer the political and financial challenges of delivering services which meet all of our needs gain from agreeing to be part of this journey? Most importantly, they have an opportunity to show to their 'masters' that the process is real. By visiting and revisiting the process of collective working, by demonstrating that they respect others' knowledge and skills, by trusting each other, things will not need to be changed because they've gone wrong, but rather because we have all recognised how we can collectively deliver sustainable services. I have found through working with some senior managers within NHS Fife that their concerns and frustrations about the lack of commitment to the process of real involvement and influence are similar to those we as users and carers express. They saw the involvement of users as a means of driving the change agenda forward in areas where they had previously been unsuccessful. In some cases they felt just as frustrated and disempowered by the 'system' as users did.

Yet they could not fully engage with users because they were constrained (about what they could say) by having to voice the organisational and/or political line on a subject, or felt they had to hold their own counsel on a subject. Therefore they were often curtailed in discussions on certain topics or were evasive when asked direct questions. This has meant that the majority of professionals don't emotionally connect with users: therefore they may be too ready to dismiss users' wants, aspirations or needs and see themselves as the only experts because they are the only ones that have the 'full picture'.

I do believe we can, through this process of recognition and sharing, break away from delivering services that meet the needs of those in power to meeting the needs of the users of services and their carers. We can work together in real partnership, sharing responsibility, recognising that we need each other, no matter what our label or position may be. They must show me that they can be trusted and that they trust me, but I need support during this journey. Recently someone said to me that they often forget I'm a user of services, because I appear a well-rounded, capable person. They now look to me to remind them when I need support to be part of their process. For me this showed that I am valued and respected, and it reinforced that I have a responsibility to be honest and trusting with those I am working alongside. Whether we drive the car, service the car, design the car, or pay for the car, we all need to be part of the process – to save time and money, and not waste valuable experience. We have so much to gain and, as I've said earlier, much more to lose.

Conclusion

As Winston Churchill once said, there are two kinds of people – the pessimist and the optimist. A pessimist sees only the obstacle, and the optimist sees the opportunity in the obstacle. I want us all to continue our journey with optimism and enthusiasm, but to do this we all need support at different times, and for different reasons. Because we are all different, each of us brings our own unique knowledge, skills and experience, gained from our own journeys. We need to trust and be trusted; we need to remind others that we are not equal partners, but that we are valuable, key partners in this process.

We need to continue our journey, questioning where we are going and looking at what we have achieved and indeed celebrating our successes. It may be that we never get to our destination, for as our aspirations change, our destinations may change. Yet I am sure that by trusting each other, acknowledging our individual strengths, and being prepared to share power in an honest way, we can all remain part of the journey, and begin to see services which will meet not only our needs, but also the needs of those tasked to deliver those services. Abraham Lincoln once said, 'If we could first know where we are, and whither we are tending, we could then better judge what to do, and how to do it.' He also said, 'I'm a slow walker, but I never walk back.' For me and others like me, this is important. I want to be able to reflect on and learn from any mistakes along the way, but I want always to continue to move forward.

We may never produce a finished painting, or reach a final destination. But I believe we have an opportunity by continuing our journey together. To look at our work, learn from our detours, stops and any breakdowns we've experienced. To all work in full partnership, no matter what label, or power, we may feel we have. To begin to see services that are designed and delivered to meet our needs and aspirations. By each of us who is involved making a commitment to continue our journey together, as valued key partners, demonstrating trust and sharing power, with whatever support we may need: we must be honest with each other. To be able to say when we feel we should and need to be involved, and equally, when we feel that we should not be involved. By being able to step back, not being at the table just to make up numbers or tick others' boxes. This honesty can lead to us all achieving the three Rs; *Real* Change, from *Real* Power, showing we have achieved *Real* Influence beyond the level of tokenism and good intentions that some of us have experienced during our journey together.

Chapter 6

Ways of Knowing

Iain Ferguson and Wendy Ager

Introduction

Several of the chapters in this book have been concerned with issues of *process*, with the ways in which service users and carers might be more involved in the selection, teaching and assessment of social work students, as well as with the factors which promote or constrain such involvement. By contrast, the focus of this chapter will be on the *content* of user experience, on service user perspectives and understandings, their 'ways of knowing'. More than a decade ago, Jones pointed to the potential of such understandings to inform professional practice when he wrote that:

> The domain of social work is compelling, important and contested. It demands and requires integrity, enquiry, debate and research. Above all, it demands new partnerships in the formation of its knowledge base and curricula which involve the users of those services and those social constituencies which have hitherto been considered as not counting. (Jones, 1996, p. 210)

Since that time, there has been a huge increase in interest, including government interest, both in service user involvement and in the knowledge base of social work. Concern with the latter is reflected, for example, in the New Labour government's creation of the Social Care Institute for Excellence (SCIE) in England and Wales and, north of the border, the Scottish Institute for Excellence in Social Work Education (SIESWE), bodies whose remit is precisely to develop social work's research and knowledge base. Both of these organisations, in different ways, have sought to involve service users and carers in this task, with the Scottish project on which this book is based one obvious example. Yet it is far from clear that the model of knowledge promoted by successive New Labour governments and currently influential within SCIE and SIESWE – evidence-based practice – is one which is capable of taking on board the experience and understandings of service users and carers in the ways which Jones proposed.

As Parton has noted, at a superficial level it seems very difficult to argue against something which seems as commonsensical as evidence-based practice, which he defines as 'the doctrine that professional practice should be based upon sound research evidence about the effectiveness of any assessment or intervention' (Parton, 2004, p. 37). Despite that, however, evidence-based practice has been subjected to a number of powerful criticisms, three of which will be briefly considered here.

Firstly, among the factors driving evidence-based approaches is the desire to reduce risk and increase certainty in social work. The report of the 21st Century Review of Social Work in Scotland, for example, discussed in Chapter 1, is explicit in making the link between greater use of research evidence and the reduction of risk:

> Because of this [i.e. the weakness of the evidence base for practice], there is a need for a national research and development strategy for social work services, which not only develops new evidence but presents existing evidence in a way which informs practice and develops the expertise in the workforce to use and evaluate its impact. *An immediate priority within this strategy should be the development of nationally agreed risk assessment tools that provide a sound underpinning for professional judgement.* (Scottish Executive, 2006, p. 55: my emphasis)

The reduction of harmful risk to service users in vulnerable situations, whether children or adults, is, of course, a goal which all would support. However, as several commentators have noted (Parton, 1996; Watson and West, 2006; Webb, 2005), while an emphasis on risk assessment frameworks may provide the illusion of being 'objective' and scientific, in reality their capacity to predict risk is limited, especially when the risks in a particular situation are considered in isolation from client need. More generally, there are problems with the rather mechanical way in which it is assumed social workers will 'apply' knowledge or empirical research evidence to practice. In this respect, as Gray and McDonald note:

> The adoption of evidence-based practice can best be understood as a continuation of long-standing attempts to deal with the ubiquity of ambiguity and uncertainty in social work. (2006, p. 12)

Yet, as they and others argue, uncertainty and contingency are at the core of social work practice. The idea that these factors can be eliminated by the 'appliance of science' rests on a false view both of social work and also of how practitioners use knowledge to make sense of people's lives and situations.

Secondly, there is the context in which evidence-based practice is being promoted. As Gray and McDonald argue, evidence-based practice is intensely political in intent (2006, p.17). It fits well with a 'modernising' agenda which sees the primary role of social work as an essentially technical one, eschewing values and a concern with inequality in favour of controlling 'risky' individuals and managing behavioural change. From a government perspective, evidence-based practice, with its claims to ideological neutrality and scientific objectivity, can play an important role in this process of creating a social work 'fit for purpose'.

Thirdly, and most importantly, there is the question of what counts as evidence. In the field of evidence-based practice, understandings of what constitutes evidence seem to rely heavily on narrow and highly traditional positivist conceptions of science, with two methods in particular – randomised control trials and meta-analyses – seen as superior to all other sources (Glasby and Beresford, 2006). Yet, as Cohen and his colleagues have pointed out, such methods have not been shown to be more reliable than other approaches; can answer only limited questions; and do not include other non-statistical forms of knowledge (Cohen *et al.*, 2004, cited in Glasby and Beresford, 2006, p. 270).

It is this last point which is of particular relevance here. For in practice, the prioritisation of these methods and the creation of a 'hierarchy of evidence' (Glasby and Beresford, 2006) can lead to the neglect of other forms of evidence which may be more, or at least equally, valid and useful for social workers. On the one hand, these might include evidence of causes of health inequalities which do not fit neatly into a narrow 'what works' framework (Pilgrim and Rogers, 2003). On the other, they may include the knowledge, experience and perspectives of service users and carers. In her chapter in this book, for example, Norma McSloy writes powerfully and movingly of how her view of 'what worked' for her son was often very different from the views of service providers.

The remainder of this chapter will look at the nature of such user knowledges and how they might inform practice. The first section draws heavily on Wendy Ager's description of the ways in which a Dundee University module on Caring sought to deepen social work students' understanding about the realities of carers' lives and perspectives. The section that follows it reflects on a research project in Glasgow which looked at how the views of people with a diagnosis of personality disorder and the views of frontline workers might inform the development of new health and social care services for this heavily stigmatised group of people.

Learning with carers

The new Masters degree at the University of Dundee, introduced in 2004, requires a high level of independent learning on the part of the student, shedding a more conventional, didactic approach to learning. In so doing, the degree explicitly sets out to blur the boundaries between practice and academic learning. Each module reflects this ethos in its own way. 'Making

Sense of the Caring Experience', the module to be discussed here, in centring the learning on service user and carer experiences and knowledge, provokes questions about knowledge and expertise. In this module, each student was linked with a family carer or someone who uses services and spent periods of time with them, totalling 24 hours. Their learning was directed by the opportunities connected to the caring responsibilities and was written up by students in three separate assignments. Students were expected to be guided by the people they were working with, both in the opportunities on offer and in the written work being completed.

Evans and Fisher (1999) suggest that 'involving service users in teaching social work brings not only immediacy to the learning but a reshaping of the notion of expertise' (p. 113). Tutors therefore saw in this module the opportunity for teaching and learning to take place firmly grounded in the lived experience of service users and carers with, most importantly, the potential for family carers and people who use services to be re-positioned as teachers or trainers in this process. As a model for social work practice, it accords a respect for service user and carer knowledge where, it is hoped, 'social workers and service users engage jointly in dialogue, exploration and mutual receptivity in the process of constructing a shared understanding which is meaningful to service users' (Smith, 2001, p. 298).

The development and co-ordination of the module

The process of module development in itself reflected a commitment to service user and carer involvement. The idea for the module originated within the university's Carer and User Group and was developed in conjunction with a lecturer in preparation for the approval process. Once approved, the module leader (a lecturer) convened a management group comprising three members of a Dundee-based organisation (PAMIS) and two lecturers. PAMIS is an organisation providing support to people with profound learning disabilities. This management group co-ordinated the recruitment of family carers and people who use services, drafted guidance and information, planned preparation of students and 'hosts' and negotiated the evaluation of the module. Formal assessment of students' written work remained the responsibility of the module leader.

Evaluating the module

Dundee staff commissioned an independent social firm to run focus groups with family carers and service users, with students, with the 'recruiting' organisations and with the lecturers and practice teachers. Individual feedback was sought from students, family carers and service users about the module, and further evidence of the impact of the experience came from the assignments which the students completed. From these different sources, staff identified a different dynamic created in the learning process – a dynamic that was sometimes seen as positive, sometimes seen as a challenge.

The feedback from family carers and people who use services indicated that they felt a strong sense of being in control of the student's time with them. They felt too that they could give the students opportunities for learning. This shift in responsibility for what is learned was reflected in a number of ways. Sometimes it was described as helping. A family carer said, 'I didn't think in terms of her helping me, but of me helping her.' Sometimes it was described as 'offering access to' or 'offering opportunities to' do something. Two service users commented in the focus group that they had offered access to activities they were involved in as activists shaping services and also to the supports they use to enable them to take on these roles. Sometimes people identified themselves as teachers or trainers in this process: 'I'm very grateful to have had this opportunity to have some input into the learning process for social work students' (Ferguson, 2005).

For those people involved as 'hosts' in this module, then, this was a good experience and there were cautious but positive hopes for the impact of the experience for students for the future.

For Dundee students it was, as Baldwin and Sadd (2006) put it in a recent paper describing a similar exercise, 'an unnerving experience' (p. 351), particularly in the initial stages of the process. Contact time was rated highly, in that being there and listening to someone's personal story was a mutually beneficial experience. However, students felt there was a lack of clarity about their role. Again this chimes with what Baldwin and Sadd (2006) say about their experience of some students feeling undermined, if their personal and professional identity is based in 'being the paid professional in possession of the expertise and the answers to service user problems' (p. 351).

Interestingly too, such feelings were not always to do with professional identity. Some students felt 'they already knew what they needed to know about caring through their own life experience, training or work experience'. They felt it was patronising to be taught about the experience of caring, given their own current or previous roles as carers. The tension here arises in the apparent denial of an identity as 'carer' in the process of learning as 'student'.

However, by virtue of being led by individual service user and carer experiences from the start within the module in Dundee, students are challenged in who is directing what. If they can learn to see that it is legitimate not to know everything (because they are the professional social worker or because they are a carer themselves), and to accept the service user or carer as the expert about their own situation and experiences, then the encounter may be more usefully experienced. Sakamoto (2005) explore this idea as 'taking a one down position' (p. 437). Tew et al. (2006) extend the idea further by illustrating how different labels do not necessarily have to create barriers to working together. Relevant and equally valued knowledge and skills shared together bring benefits and enrich learning. One carer who is learning to be a social worker must learn to put themselves into a position to learn from another carer.

Involvement in written assignments was another key feature of this module. In looking at comments, it is apparent that different values were brought to bear on the work achieved. Family carers and service users enjoyed being involved and particularly emphasised the accuracy of presentations by students. They appreciated the care, respect and accountability that this demonstrated. Lecturers by contrast valued a balance struck between the need to illustrate the 'journey through care' of the service user and/or carer with the need for students to demonstrate academic competence. This difference in the relative values assigned to students' work hints at the potential tension arising from attempts to explicitly blur boundaries.

As noted earlier, formal assessment of students' work remained the responsibility of the module leader. Individual feedback to students by service users and carers was part of the formative assessment for students. However, it did not contribute to the summative evaluation of students, signalling a difficulty in fully including carer and service user perspectives in the formal assessment process.

This module is now in its second year; the management group has expanded to take on board area managers of the Princess Royal Trust for Carers in order to add to the recruitment and support of the carers involved, and alterations have been made to the timing. The quest to further integrate learning and assessment based on service user and carer knowledge and expertise will inevitably challenge institutional academic practice.

Lacking in insight? The views of people with a diagnosis of personality disorder

The second example of the potential of service user knowledges to inform health and social work practice involves a piece of research conducted in 2002-3 into the perspectives and experiences of a group of mental health service users who are often seen as 'difficult' or 'hard to engage with': people with a diagnosis of personality disorder (Ferguson et al., 2003). The study was commissioned by Greater Glasgow Primary Care Trust in 2002 as a basis for developing their services with this group of service users. This was a small-scale qualitative study and the usual caveats about the dangers of generalising too much from its findings are therefore both necessary and appropriate. That said, some of the key findings have been replicated in other research in this area (Castillo, 2003) and in subsequent research by us (Ferguson et al., 2005). This would suggest they merit consideration in the development of services, not least given the paucity of other user views research with this group of service users.

The research was based on interviews with ten service users (eight females, two males) recruited through mental health resource centres. These individuals were suggested by resource centre staff on the basis that they had previously been given a diagnosis of personality disorder by a psychiatrist. Twelve service provider respondents from the Greater Glasgow area were also interviewed, including psychiatrists, psychologists, community psychiatric nurses, occupational therapists, social workers, and staff from voluntary organisations. The research was guided throughout by an Advisory Group which included service users with a diagnosis of personality disorder, as well as some professionals. Following discussion with the Advisory Group, it was agreed that the research would address the following areas:

- understandings of personality disorder and the perceived usefulness of this term;
- main problems in living experienced by people with personality disorders;
- strategies and supports employed to address these difficulties;
- helpfulness of existing mental health services and identification of good practice;
- understandings of risk;
- helpful responses to risk.

Here, for reasons of space, discussion of the research findings will focus on only two of these areas: understandings of personality disorder as a diagnosis, and problems in living.

Making sense of personality disorder

Personality disorder has been included as a form of mental disorder in the Mental Health (Scotland) Act 2003, in contrast to the main legislation previously in force in Scotland, where only one form of personality disorder, usually known as 'psychopathy', was referred to (and then only indirectly). Given the potential implications of such inclusion for the civil liberties of those involved, it would not be unreasonable to expect a fairly high degree of consensus as to what this diagnosis actually involved. In fact, as Tyrer *et al.* have noted, personality disorder is a highly contested diagnosis within the professional mental health community (Tyrer *et al.*, 1991). The first part of this study therefore was concerned with exploring how both professional and service user respondents saw this term and their views on its perceived usefulness as a diagnosis.

In their answers, service provider respondents fell into three main groups: first, those who accepted broad psychiatric classifications of personality disorders but felt there was a need for more training in accurate diagnosis; second, those who drew on a social deviance model and saw personality disorder primarily as a form of labelling; and a third group who saw people with this diagnosis as experiencing 'difficulties in living' similar to or more extreme than those experienced by most people but with less resources of every type – emotional, social and financial – to deal with them.

Perceptions of the usefulness of this diagnosis tended to reflect these understandings of the term. Thus, members of the first group felt that psychiatric classifications of personality disorder were useful but only if used 'accurately', i.e. not in a pejorative way. A second group was unhappy with the term but resigned to using it on the pragmatic grounds that, whatever its limitations, it was the accepted term within health services dominated by a medical model. A third group, however, was much more negative about this diagnosis, seeing it as being of doubtful validity, encouraging therapeutic pessimism, leading to exclusion from services and extremely stigmatising, and felt therefore that it should be abandoned.

Given this ambivalence surrounding the term, there was unsurprisingly a similar lack of consensus over whether or not the diagnosis should be shared with service users. By contrast, amongst the service user respondents, there were considerable similarities in views and experiences. The majority, for example, had 'no idea' or little idea' what the term meant:

> I don't know and I have never been told what it means. I think it's because of my upbringing and things that my personality has not turned out as well as it could have done. There is something wrong with my personality and it is disordered in some way.

Several had previously been given more than one other diagnosis and felt that a personality disorder diagnosis had only been given when no other fitted:

> I don't really know because it's like over the years I have had so many diagnoses. As far as I know the only reason I have been diagnosed with a personality disorder is because I self-harm but as for anything else I don't know. No one has ever explained it to me.

Others queried the supposedly 'permanent' nature of the condition, feeling that they coped better at certain times than at others:

> The other thing I understand about personality disorder is that it is a permanent thing. But I actually find that sometimes I am better and don't cut a lot and everything is going OK and I am quite happy and other times I am frantic, going mental and cutting all the time and burning and doing all sorts of things.

This lack of clarity about what the term meant was perhaps not surprising, since a majority stated that, although they were aware of their diagnosis, it had never been explained to them:

> [I was told] about 6 or 7 years ago. I have just been told that I have got a personality disorder. Nobody has ever sat me down and said this is what it means and why I have got it.

Others stated that they had discovered their diagnosis by accident – for example, on the back of a government benefit form, on a discharge certificate, or by glancing through a medical file. Unsurprisingly, this increased their anxieties and sense of pessimism. By contrast, some service users involved in particular treatment programmes (such as forms of cognitive behaviour therapy) *did* have an understanding of what was meant by borderline personality disorder and, while they disliked the term, were nevertheless able to use it as a basis for requesting services.

Half of the service user respondents stated that they disliked the term very much. It was seen as a derogatory term and as a label which excluded people from services on the basis of not having a mental illness:

> I don't like it. It makes me feel a bit of a freak, it makes me feel different. It is a horrible term for someone. It must be helpful for the doctors or they wouldn't use it.

> I don't think it's such a good term anyway. I think it should be changed to something to do with feelings and emotions. I can't think of an exact term but something that doesn't mean attention-seeking behaviour, that means that it's a very, very difficult life for them to lead.

By contrast, a small number preferred to have *any* diagnosis than no diagnosis, while others felt that the condition, not the label, was the major problem.

A number of issues arise from the above findings. First of all, there is a certain irony in the fact that at the very point when there is growing concern in both the professional and service user communities (Pilgrim, 2001; Castillo, 2003) over the validity, reliability and stigmatising impact of the diagnosis of personality disorder, it should for the first time be firmly entrenched in mental health law in Scotland.

A further drawback of the term noted above is that, due to its imprecision and devastating implications for self-esteem, several clinicians in this study felt unable to share the diagnosis with service users. While this is understandable, service users felt even more disempowered by the lack of information surrounding this condition since it prevented them from gaining any sense of mastery of the condition. In recognition of this, one outcome of the study was the award of further funding in Greater Glasgow to allow for the production of a brochure by a researcher and service users explaining the different perspectives on personality disorder.

Problems in living

Historically, individuals with a diagnosis of personality disorder have often been perceived by mental health professionals as 'difficult' to work with (Lewis and Appleby, 1988). Recent research into the attitudes of nurses towards people with a diagnosis of borderline personality disorder suggests that such negative attitudes persist (Deans and Meocevic, 2006). One service provider respondent in this study, when asked to identify the main problems experienced by this group of service users, commented:

> Interpersonal difficulties, that's something that staff find difficult. They can be demanding and they tend often not to engage or not to do things as you're asked or within a time frame or various things so they're perhaps not the most likeable of clients, you know. I mean you think well OK Jimmy Bloggs; I really like him because he comes every day of when he's told to come in and does exactly what I tell him and whatever.

What factors might lie at the root of the behaviours that staff experience as difficult? In fact, difficulties in managing relationships, both personal and professional, was identified by both service users and service providers as the main problem experienced by people with this label. For one service user:

> Having relationships with people, trusting people and trusting doctors and professionals as well. That is one of the hardest things.

There was recognition from another user of the ways in which these difficulties could cause problems in relationships with professionals:

> I find it difficult negotiating with people. If I miss an appointment, I am very, very apologetic and profusely apologise. I do give myself a hard time.

As regards the origins of these difficulties, both sets of respondents emphasised the significance of life events, and particularly early life events:

> I have had a rotten life. I was abused in every form. The abuse was terrible then I became an addict and my drinking got worse. My husband was an alcoholic and I used to dread him coming home at night. I think I started self-harming when I was 5. I grew up not knowing when my birthday was.

Such events were perceived as having impacted on individuals in two main ways. Firstly, they gave rise to very powerful and painful feelings which were difficult to manage and control; secondly, they undermined people's capacity for trust. In relation to feelings, one service provider respondent commented:

> I think that the biggest difficulty is emotional and the emotional area of their life. They struggle to deal with their emotions and I think in turn that means that they struggle in relationships, all kinds

of relationships in dealing with people, and I also think they have huge problems with dealing with stress which again links to the emotional problems.

For one service user:

> One minute you can be OK, the next you're going really, really down and like ma case, I'm awfy sensitive to the silliest things like stress.

A clinician suggested that:

> Trust, I would say almost whichever category of personality disorder, some trust issue with people is an important one and often you will find there have been trust issues in childhood, whether parents splitting up or abuse or things like that. So yes, it is very common for there to be experiences that at the very least magnified their natural traits.

One consequence of these relationship difficulties, seldom mentioned in the professional literature but identified by service users in this study as a major issue for them, was loneliness. (In fact a recent MIND study [MIND, 2004] found social isolation and loneliness to be a major problem amongst people with mental health problems generally.)

> I feel lonely. I am quite isolated. I don't have anybody. I can't have friends because they all die. I don't want to go through that again. I don't let anybody in, I just like to sit by the kitchen window and watch what is happening outside.

That loneliness and sense of isolation was compounded by the stigma and lack of understanding associated with mental ill-health, and especially personality disorder. Several respondents confessed to often feeling like 'freaks':

> I feel as though I have mental illness stamped on my forehead, as though everybody will know I am mentally ill. So I don't like going out without my carer.

> The press make out that we're schizos, loonies, we're going to hurt people, and it's the people round about that hurt us.

Both sets of respondents acknowledged that forming trusting relationships was a considerable challenge for this group of people. However, a number of things were identified that could assist in this process. Firstly, consistency of worker. Several service users spoke of the difficulty of having to re-tell their story again and again to different workers and of the time it took to build up a trusting relationship. By contrast, where there was consistency and such a relationship was established, this was a major factor in reducing risk of harm. Secondly, the need for greater support, supervision and training for workers was stressed by both users and professionals. Again, both groups acknowledged that there were significant differences between individual workers in their ability to be helpful to this group of service users, differences which seemed to be related to possession of a theoretical framework, personal self-awareness, understanding of stigma and value base. It was clear that while some workers found this a very difficult client group to work with, others took a more positive approach:

> I think the tendency is for it to bring up the same feelings in you as they feel. A projection of feelings because they feel helpless and so if you are not getting anywhere with them because they feel helpless, then you end up a bit helpless as well and you can feel angry and irritable as well ... it is how you deal with these feelings that can determine the extent to which you can actually be helpful.

Finally, while some service users found one-to-one therapeutic work helpful, it needs to be underpinned by the creation of appropriate forms of social support and social networks. As mentioned above, the issue of loneliness and social isolation was a major one for several of these respondents (and, as a subsequent study found, was one factor in the breakdown of tenancies for homeless people with some form of personality disorder who had previously lived in hostel accommodation (Ferguson *et al.*, 2005). There is a long tradition within social work of community development and social networking approaches which has been eclipsed in recent years by the dominance of care management and individualised approaches. These findings suggest the relevance of these earlier approaches in addressing problems of isolation and loneliness.

Conclusions

In this chapter, we have suggested that currently influential notions of evidence-based practice not only risk undermining traditional social work concerns with values and issues of inequality but may also devalue the specific knowledges, the 'ways of knowing', of people who use services and of those who care for them. By contrast, the two examples discussed above point to some of the ways in which such knowledges can lead to very different – and potentially much more productive – relationships between service users, carers and social work students and professionals, as well as informing the development of new, more accessible services. At the very least, the positive evidence of such initiatives should reinforce the determination of all those who are concerned with addressing the needs of these groups to ensure that their voices are not silenced or excluded.

CHAPTER 7

Concluding Thoughts:
Frustrations and Possibilities

Iain Ferguson

While each of the contributions to this collection is very different, it is possible to discern two themes which run through all of them. The first theme relates to the *frustrations* around user involvement, some of which stem from the failure, and occasionally unwillingness, of professionals and policy-makers to hear what service users and carers are saying. This failure is sometimes compounded by a limited understanding of partnership, with power remaining very firmly in the hands of the service providers and professionals, and also by the persistence of tokenism, in the sense of cosmetic involvement which leaves practice, services and professional education unchanged. It is often these factors which, despite the 'good intentions' of those involved, can create resentment and despair on the part of service users and carers and cause some to withdraw from the whole process. The roots of some of these frustrations and constraints in consumerist, 'top-down' models of user involvement are explored in several chapters in this book. This is not, of course, an isolated finding. As the authors of another research study of user involvement have noted:

> There has been an increasing emphasis in recent years on user involvement in health and social care policy and practice. However it has come in for growing questioning. Service providers and researchers have begun to ask what evidence there is that it improves services. Service users and their organisations have raised the issue of what they are actually able to achieve by their involvement and to question the usefulness of getting involved. (Branfield *et al.*, 2006, p. 1)

There is also, however, a second, more positive theme which emerges from these chapters. It is the recognition of the *potential* of user and carer involvement, the possibility of reconstructing professional practice, social work and social care services, and professional education, on a very different basis. Writing in the mid-1990s, Jones pointed to that potential in the realm of professional social work education when he wrote that the complexity of social work:

> demands new partnerships in the formation of its knowledge base and curricula which involve the users of those services and those social constituencies which have hitherto been considered as not counting. (Jones, 1996, p. 210)

The recognition that user and carer involvement in social work education creates the possibility of developing new frameworks for practice, services and education was voiced by several contributors in the evaluation of the SIESWE project, Project 3.3. One social work tutor commented on her experience of discussing her teaching with service users as part of that project:

> Just by virtue of sitting talking to a service user and being aware of their articulacy, the strength of what they have to say, it actually makes you much more motivated to bring people in ... The very process of sitting in front of the service user and having that conversation makes you realise you want them to be having that conversation with students that you are working with. (Quoted in Ferguson, 2005)

Similarly, there was a recognition amongst service user and carer participants in the evaluation that tokenism can be overcome, with several expressing appreciation of the conscious effort made by the staff most closely involved to ensure that change was both taking place and was seen to be taking place.

The overall message which emerges from these chapters, then, is contradictory but also hopeful in that it suggests that, given certain conditions, the potential for service user and carer involvement to enrich and enhance social work education can be realised. In these concluding pages, I shall discuss two of the core conditions which have emerged from Project 3.3 as essential for effective involvement: the existence of *demonstrable trust* and the *acknowledgement of power differentials*.

Demonstrable trust

In their respective chapters, both John Dow and Norma McSloy emphasise the importance for effective service user and carer involvement not only of trust but of *demonstrable* trust (Shemmings and Shemmings, 1995). Their reflections suggest that there are three elements to demonstrable trust. First, clarity about the agendas of those involved. As analysts such as Arnstein (1969) and Cockburn (1977) recognised more than thirty years ago, different agendas, not all of them benign, may underlie the invitation to 'participate'. Service users and carers need to know that in contributing their time and experience, these valuable assets are not being used to meet the objectives of agendas to which they have not signed up. They need to be able to trust the motives of those involved.

One aspect of this concerns the 'top-down' origins of much current user involvement. Consumerist models of user involvement are, of course, at the heart of New Labour's programme of welfare reform:

> I am not talking about modest further reorganization but something quite different and more fundamental. We are proposing to put an entirely different dynamic in place to drive our public services: one where the service will be driven not by the government or by the managers but by the user – the patient, the parent, the pupil and the law abiding citizen. The service will continue to be free, but it will be a high quality consumer service to fit their needs in the same way as the best services do in other areas of life. (Tony Blair, 2004)

Whatever the merits of such 'top-down' models of involvement, an obvious downside is that those charged with implementing the policy at lower levels may be doing so primarily because the 'user involvement' box needs to be ticked. For example, both in Scotland and also south of the Border, evidence of service user and carer involvement in all aspects of social work education was a condition of validation of new social work degree programmes within universities. While the vast majority of staff members were in fact keen to develop this aspect of their work, the lack of any additional funding (in Scotland at least) to make this possible has inevitably meant that the development of such involvement has had to be fitted into the schedules of already busy staff. The danger then becomes that the requirement for such involvement is simply experienced as one more demand from management which is not backed up by additional time or resources. Building trusting relationships with service users and carers takes time. If that time is not made available to the staff involved, then it is not hard to see how users and carers will quickly conclude that there is a lack of commitment to such involvement and vote with their feet. By contrast, Chapter 2 by Maggie Gee and Mo McPhail shows just how much can be achieved where additional funds and staffing are allocated to user involvement, in this case to assist the work of the University of Dundee Project 3.3 demonstration project.

Second, there is the issue of process. Again, several of the contributors make reference to the efforts made within this project to ensuring that all voices were being heard and everyone's concerns taken on board. Similarly, in the writing of the current book, it was important to try and find ways in which the experience of the different contributors could be most effectively expressed. Creating a culture where difference can be expressed and the value of different perspectives taken on board is not easy, nor is the process always a consensual one. As a minimum, it requires genuine respect on all sides.

The third aspect of demonstrable trust is evidence of outcomes. Again, people are unlikely to give up their time unless they see evidence of change.

In this respect, the service users and carers involved in this project were mainly positive. Commenting on their input into the teaching programme at Dundee University, for example, one service user noted that;

> Despite some of my less than positive feedback I do feel we are beginning to make a change around how users and carers can support change and help the professionals in this process. I am really pleased that students have commented on how useful our input as users and carers has been to them in assessing how they will approach working with their client groups. (Cited in Ferguson, 2005)

Awareness of power differentials

Alongside trust, the issue of power was also one raised by most contributors to this book. In many arenas where service users and carers are involved with health and social work professionals, power is very often 'the elephant in the corner' – seldom mentioned but its presence and operation blindingly obvious to the service users and carers present, despite the rhetoric of 'partnership'. Within consumerist models of involvement in particular, seeing the user as a 'customer' tends to obscure the very real differences – in terms of purchasing power, status and access to information and knowledge – between users of social work services and the model customer of economic textbooks. In addition, issues of power arise at every stage of the process of user involvement and include such issues as agenda-setting, provision of information, culture of meetings, familiarity with procedures and decision-making.

As the Guidelines for Good Practice (Ager *et al.*, 2006) highlight, there is much that can be done to reduce these power differentials and create a more level playing field for service users and carers involved in social work education and service development generally. It would be naïve, however, to assume that power inequalities can easily be wished away or to deny the fact that, in some situations, conflicts of interest will arise between the different agendas of those providing services on the one hand and those seeking to influence the shape and direction of these services on the other. In such situations good practice in user involvement, as in social work more generally, would seem to involve a frank acknowledgement of these differentials and open negotiation over what can and what cannot be changed.

More generally, if, as some writers have argued, service users and carers should be seen as a type of 'new social movement' (Barnes, 1997), then the whole experience of social movements in the twentieth century, from the suffragettes at the beginning of the century to the disability movement at the end, is that simply asking for more power and more rights from those in power has rarely, if ever, been an effective strategy. It is usually only when such movements have developed their own power bases, strategies and tactics, often in alliance with other social movements, that they have begun to achieve real change (Lavalette and Mooney, 2000), including exerting a significant influence on social work and social care (Thompson, 2002). As David Harvey has suggested, 'true empowerment must be won by struggles from below and not given out of largesse from above' (cited in Mayo, 1994, p. 54).

In respect of the national network of service users and carers, Scottish Voices, this does not mean that group members should not seize whatever opportunities are made available to them to influence the future direction of social work education. As Harris has observed, much of the progress that user organisations have made over the past decade has resulted from them taking the rhetoric of consumerism seriously and demanding that government agencies translate words into deeds (Harris, 2004). Two caveats are necessary however. First, it is crucial that such involvement is properly funded and supported. Without such funding and support, cynicism is likely to set in very quickly.

Second, it implies the need for independent, collective organisation. The discussion of the national network (Chapter 2) suggests that 'vigilance is needed to ensure that service users and carers are not used as political pawns' in areas of intra-professional disagreement or to meet other political or agency agendas. Vigilance *is* important, but so too is the development of independent service user and carer forums and structures where the best way to build the national group can be discussed and debated, perhaps with the support of workers or others whom those involved have identified as 'allies'. The development of such independent organisation need not conflict with the development of a partnership approach. On the contrary, the more that service users and carers are able to meet the professionals and politicians on their own terms, the more effective such partnership is likely to be. Again, the need for such organisation emerges not just from this study. One finding of the research referred to above, which involved discussion with 126 service users in different parts of the UK, was the need for more effective networking between user organisations. One respondent commented:

> We need a collective national voice. If we are to succeed we need stronger grass roots activism. (Branfield *et al.*, 2006, p. 2)

In conclusion, then, the development of meaningful service user and carer involvement in social work education will only take place if demonstrable trust of the type discussed above is consciously fostered and power differentials frankly acknowledged and actively minimised. The lesson of this book, however, and of the project on which it is based, is that if these conditions can be met, then the rewards for a social work profession which is sorely in need of rejuvenation and renewal can be very considerable indeed.

References

Ager, W. (2004) in SIESWE (2004) *Scottish Voices: Service Users and Carers at the Heart of Social Work Education*. Available from URL: www.sieswe.org/node/185 (accessed 10 July 2007)

Ager, W. (2005) *Service User and Carer Feedback in Placement Reports*. Available from URL: www.sieswe.org/docs/IA33EvalPilot5.pdf

Ager, W. and Gee, M. (2004) *Service User and Carer Involvement in Social Work Education: A Practice Audit*. Available from URL: www.sieswe.org/docs/IA33PracAudit.pdf

Ager, W., Dow, J. and Gee, M. (2005) 'Grassroots networks: a model for promoting the influence of social work users and carers in social work education', *Social Work Education*, Vol. 24, No. 4, pp. 469–79

Ager, W., Dow, J., Gee, M., Ferguson, I., McPhail, M. and McSloy, N. (2006) *Service User and Carer Involvement in Social Work Education: Good Practice Guidelines*. Available from URL: www.sieswe.org/files/IA33GoodPracticeGuidelines.pdf

Allam, S., Blyth, S., Fraser, A., Hodgson, S., Howes, J., Repper, J. and Newman, A. (2004) 'Our experience of collaborative research: service users, carers and researchers work together to evaluate an assertive outreach service', *Journal of Psychiatric and Mental Health Nursing*, Vol. 11, No. 3, pp. 368–78

Arnstein, S. R. (1969) 'A ladder of participation', *Journal of the American Institute of Planners*, Vol. 35, No. 4, pp. 216–24

Baldwin, M. and Sadd, J. (2006) 'Allies with attitude! Service users, academics and social service agency staff learning how to share power in running social work education courses', *Social Work Education*, Vol. 25, No. 4, pp. 348–452

Barbera, F. (2005) 'Social networks, collective action and public policy: the embeddedness idea reconsidered', in Koniordos, S. (ed.) (2005) *Networks, Trust and Social Capital*, Aldershot: Ashgate, pp. 119–42

Barnes, M. (1997) *Care, Communities and Citizens*, London: Longman

Barnes, M., Carpenter, J. and Dickson, C. (2006) 'The outcomes of partnerships with mental health service users in interprofessional education: a case study', *Health and Social Care in the Community*, Vol. 14, No. 5, pp. 426–35

Begum, N. (2006) *Doing it for Themselves: Participation and Black and Minority Ethnic Service Users*, Bristol, Policy Press

Beresford, P. (2006) 'Service user values: the rights-based approach to social care', in *Affirming our Value Base in Social Work and Social Care Conference Guide*, Community Care, Nottingham Trent University

Beresford, P. (2007) 'User involvement, research and health inequalities: developing new directions', *Health and Social Care in the Community*, Vol. 15, No. 4, pp. 306–12

Beresford, P. and Branfield, P. (2006) 'Developing inclusive partnerships: user defined outcomes, networking and knowledge – a case study', *Health and Social Care in the Community*, Vol. 14, No. 5, pp. 436–44

Beresford, P. and Croft, S. (1993) *Citizen Involvement: A Practical Guide to Change*, Basingstoke: Macmillan Press

Beresford, P. and Croft, S. (2003) 'Involving service users in management: citizenship, access and support', in Reynolds, J. (ed.) (2003) *The Managing Care Reader*, London: Routledge, pp. 21–8

Beresford, P. with Page, L. and Stevens, A. (1994) *Changing the Culture: Involving Service Users in Social Work Education*, CCETSW Paper 32.2, London: CCETSW

Blair, T. (2004) Speech on public services delivered at Guy's and St Thomas' Hospital London on 23 June 2004. Full speech available from URL: http://news.bbc.co.uk/1/hi/uk_politics/3833345.stm

Boylan, J., Dalrymple, J. and Ing, P. (2000) 'Let's do it! Advocacy , young people and social work education', *Social Work Education*, Vol. 19, No. 6, pp. 553–63

Branfield, F. and Beresford, P. with Andrews, E. J., Chambers, P., Staddon, P., Wise, G. and Williams-Finlay, B. (2006) *Making User Involvement Work: Supporting Service User Involvement and Knowledge*, York: Joseph Rowntree Foundation

Branfield, F., Beresford, P. and Levin, E. (2007) *Common Aims: A Strategy to Support Service User Involvement in Social Work Education*, London, SCIE

Braye, S. (2000) 'Participation and involvement in social care: an overview', in Kemshall, H. and Littlechild, R. (eds) (2000) *User Involvement and Participation in Social Care: Research Informing Practice*, London: Jessica Kingsley, pp. 9–28

Brooker, C., James, A. and Readhead, E. (2003) *National Continuous Quality Improvement Tool for Mental Health Education*, Durham and York, Northern Centre for Mental Health

Carr, S. (2004) *Has Service User Participation Made a Difference to Social Care Services?* SCIE Position Paper 3. London: SCIE

Carr, S. (2007) 'Participation, power, conflict and change: theorizing dynamics of service user participation in the social care system of England and Wales', *Critical Social Policy*, Vol. 27, No. 2, pp. 266–76

Castillo, H. (2003) *Personality Disorder: Temperament or Trauma?* London: Jessica Kingsley

Cockburn, C. (1977) *The Local State*, London: Pluto

Cohen, A. M., Stavri, P. Z. and Hersh, W. R. (2004) 'A Categorization and Analysis of the Criticism of Evidence-based Medicine', *Journal of Medical Informatics*, Vol. 73, No. 1, pp. 35–43

Cooley, A. and Lawrence, Z. (2006) *Rewards and Recognition: The Principles and Practice of Service User Payment and Reimbursement in Health and Social Care*, London: Department of Health

Cowden, S. and Singh, G. (2007) 'The user: friend, foe or fetish? A critical exploration of user involvement in health and social care', *Critical Social Policy*, Vol. 27, No. 1, pp. 5–23

Crisp, B., Green Lister, P. and Dutton, K. (2006) 'Not just social work academics: the involvement of others in the assessment of social work students', *Social Work Education*, Vol. 25, No. 7, pp. 723–34

Croft, S. and Beresford, P. (1993) *Getting Involved: A Practical Manual*, London: Open Services Project and JRF

CU Group (2005) CU Annual Report, University of Dundee, available from Maggie Gee, email m.gee@dundee.ac.uk

Curran, T. (1997) 'Power, participation and post modernism: user and practitioner participation in mental health social work education', *Social Work Education*, Vol. 16, No. 3, pp. 21–36

Deans, C. and Meocevic, E. (2006) 'Attitudes of registered psychiatric nurses towards patients diagnosed with borderline personality disorder', *Contemporary Nurse*, Vol. 21, No. 1, pp. 43–9

Evans, C. and Fisher, M. (1999) *Evaluation and Social Work Practice*, London: Sage

Ferguson, I. (2003) 'Mental health and social work', in Baillie, D., Cameron, K., Cull, L-A, Roche, J. and West, J. (eds) (2003) *Social Work and the Law in Scotland*, Basingstoke: Palgrave Macmillan/OU Press

Ferguson, I. (2005) 'Evaluation report of the University of Dundee Demonstration Project'. available from URL: www.sieswe.org/docs/IA33EvalDemo.pdf

Ferguson, I., Barclay, A. and Stalker, K. (2003) *'It's a Difficult Life to Lead': Supporting People with Personality Disorder: Service User and Provider Perspectives*, University of Stirling. Available from URL: www.dass.stir.ac.uk/staff/SupportingPeople.htm

Ferguson, I., Petrie, M. and Stalker, K. (2005) *Developing Accessible Services for Homeless People with Severe Mental Distress and Behavioural Difficulties*, Department of Applied Social Science, University of Stirling

Fisher, M. (2002) 'The Social Care Institute for Excellence: the role of a national institute in developing knowledge and practice in social care', *Social Work and Social Sciences*, Vol. 10, No. 2, pp. 6–34

Forbat, L. (2005) *Talking about Care*, Bristol: Policy Press

Forbes, J. and Sashidharan, S. P. (1997) 'User involvement in services: incorporation or challenge?', *British Journal of Social Work*, Vol. 27, No. 4, pp. 481–98

Gee, M. (2005) 'Evaluation Report: Reflective Practice Skills 2'. Available from URL: www.sieswe.org/docs/IA33EvalPilot2.pdf

Glasby, J. and Beresford, P. (2006) 'Who knows best? Evidence-based practice and the service user contribution', *Critical Social Policy*, Vol. 26, No. 1, pp. 268–84

Goss, S. and Miller, C. (1995) *From Margin to Mainstream: Developing Service User- and Carer-Centred Community Care*. York: Joseph Rowntree Foundation

Gray, M. and McDonald, C. (2006) 'Pursuing good practice? The limits of evidence-based practice', *Journal of Social Work*, Vol. 6, No. 1, pp. 7–20

Harris, J. (2003) *The Social Work Business: The State of Welfare*, Oxon: Routledge

Harris, J. (2004) 'Consumerism: social development or social delimitation?', *International Social Work*, Vol. 47, No. 4, pp. 533–42

Humphreys, C. (2005) 'Involvement in social work education: a case example', *Social Work Education*, Vol. 24, No. 7, pp. 757–803

Jones, C. (1996) 'Anti-intellectualism and the peculiarities of British social work education', in Parton, N. (ed.) (1996) *Social Theory, Social Change and Social Work*, London: Routledge, pp. 190–210

Kemshall, H. and Littlechild, R. (eds) (2000) *User Involvement and Participation in Social Care: Research Informing Practice*, London: Jessica Kingsley

Koniordos, S. (ed.) (2005) *Networks, Trust and Social Capital*, Aldershot: Ashgate

Kovalainen, A. (2005) 'Social capital, trust and dependency,' in Koniordos, S. (ed.) (2005) *Networks, Trust and Social Capital*, Aldershot: Ashgate, pp. 71–90

Lavalette, M. and Mooney, G. (2000) (eds) *Class Struggle and Social Welfare*, London: Routledge

Levin, E. (2004) *Involving Service Users and Carers in Social Work Education*, London: SCIE

Lewis, G. and Appleby, L. (1988) 'Personality disorder: the patients psychiatrists dislike', *British Journal of Psychiatry*, Vol. 153, pp. 44–9

Manthorpe, J. (2000) 'Developing carers' contributions to social work training', *Social Work Education*, Vol. 19, No. 1, pp. 19–27

Mayer, J. and Timms, N. (1970) *The Client Speaks*, London: Routledge and Kegan Paul

Mayo, M. (1994) *Communities and Caring: The Mixed Economy of Welfare*, London: Macmillan

McPhail, M. A. (2005) 'Consultation report'. Available from URL: www.sieswe.org/docs/NGI-finalreport.pdf

MIND (2004) *Not Alone? Isolation and Mental Distress*, London: MIND

Montgomery, M. (1995) *An Introduction to Language and Society*, London: Routledge

Newman, J., Barnes, M., Sullivan, H. and Knops, A. (2004) 'Public participation and collaborative governance', *Journal of Social Policy*, Vol. 33, No. 2, pp. 203–23

Parton, N. (1996) 'Social work, risk and "the blaming system"', in N. Parton (ed.) (1996) *Social Theory, Social Change and Social Work*, London: Routledge

Parton, N. (2004) 'Post-theories for practice: challenging the dogmas', in Davies, L. and Leonard, P. (eds) *Social Work in a Corporate Era: Practices of Power and Resistance*, Aldershot: Ashgate

Pilgrim, D. (2001) 'Disordered personalities and disordered concepts', *Journal of Mental Health*, Vol. 10, No. 3, pp. 253–65

Pilgrim, D. and Rogers, A. (2003) 'Mental disorder and violence: an empirical picture in context', *Journal of Mental Health*, Vol. 12, No. 1, pp. 7–18

Pithouse, A. and Williamson, H. (1997) *Engaging the Service User in Welfare Services*', Birmingham, Venture Press

Powell, F. (2001) *The Politics of Social Work*, London, Sage

Postle, K. and Beresford, P. (2007) 'Capacity building and the re-conception of political participation: a role for social care workers?', *British Journal of Social Work*, Vol. 37, No. 1, pp. 143–58

Ramon, S., Fox, J. and Anghel, R. (2006) 'Towards overcoming barriers: evaluating the impact of involving users and carers in a BA Social Work Programme', JSWEC Conference Workshop July 2006. Available from URL: www.swapexternal.soton.ac.uk/jswec2006/presentations.asp

Rosenkopf, I., Metui, A. and Varghese, G. (2001) 'From the bottom up? Technical committee activity and formation', *Administrative Science Quarterly*, December, pp. 748–72

Sadd, J. (2004) in SIESWE (2004) *Scottish Voices: Service Users and Carers at the Heart of Social Work Education*, Dundee, www.sieswe.org

Sakamoto, I. (2005) 'Use of critical consciousness in anti-oppressive social work practice: disentangling power dynamics at personal and structural levels', *British Journal of Social Work*, Vol. 35, No. 4, pp. 435–52

Scheyett, A. and Diehl, M. J. (2004) 'Walking our talk in social work education: partnering with consumers of mental health services', *Social Work Education*, Vol. 23, No. 4, pp. 435–50

Scheyett, A. and McCarthy, E. (2006) 'Working together: an ongoing collaboration between a school of social work and advocates for families of people with mental illnesses', *Social Work Education*, Vol. 25, No. 6, pp. 623–32

Scottish Executive (2000) *The Same as You*, Edinburgh: Scottish Executive

Scottish Executive (2006) *Changing Lives: Report of the 21st Century Social Work Review*, Edinburgh: Scottish Executive

Scottish Executive (2007) 'Changing Lives: Newsletter', (March). Available from URL: www. socialworkscotland.org.uk

Seden, J. (2007) 'Editorial', *British Journal of Social Work*, Vol. 37, No. 1, pp. 1–4

Shemmings, D. and Shemmings, Y. (1995) 'Defining participative practice in health and welfare,' in Jack, R. (ed.) (1995) *Empowerment in Community Care*, London: Chapman and Hall, pp. 43–58

Shirato, T. and Yell, S. (2000) *Communication and Culture: An Introduction*, London: Sage

SIESWE (2003) 'SIESWE briefing paper', Dundee: SIESWE

SIESWE, (2004) *Scottish Voices: Service Users and Carers at the Heart of Social Work Education*, Dundee, www.sieswe.org

SIESWE (2006) *Consultation Report of the National Group of Influence*, Dundee: SIESWE

Smith, C. (2001) 'Trust and confidence: possibilities for social work in high modernity', *British Journal of Social Work*, Vol. 31, No. 2, pp. 287–305

Stalker, K.(ed.) (2003) 'Reconceptualising Work with "Carers"'. London, Jessica Kingsley

Stevens, S. and Tanner, D. (2006) 'Involving service users in the teaching and learning of social work students: reflections on experience, *Social Work Education*, Vol. 25, No. 4, pp. 360–71

Swift, P. (2002) *Service Users' Views of Social Workers: A Review of the Literature Undertaken on Behalf of the Department of Health, London*', Institute for Applied Health and Social Policy, Kings College

Taylor, I., Sharland, E., Sebba, J., Leriche, P., with Keep, E. and Orr, D. (2006) *The Learning, Teaching and Assessment of Partnership in Social Work Education*, London: SCIE

Tew, J. (ed.) (2005) *Social Perspectives in Mental Health: Developing Social Models to Understand and Work with Mental Distress*, London: Jessica Kingsley

Tew, G., Patel, R., Hendry, S., Haines A. and Salmon, L. (2006) 'Expectations, identities and labels: reflections on learning together', unpublished workshop paper presented at JSWEC Conference Workshop, July 2006

Thompson, N. (2002) 'Social movements, social justice and social work', *British Journal of Social Work*, Vol. 32, No. 6, pp. 711–22

Turner, M. and Beresford, P. (2005) *Contributing on Equal Terms. Service User Involvement and the Benefits System*, Bristol: Policy Press

Turner, M. and Shaping Our Lives National User Network (2002) *Guidelines for Involving Service Users in Social Work Education*, Southampton: Social Policy and Social Work Learning and Teaching Support. Available from URL: www.swap.ac.uk

Tyler, G. (2006) 'Addressing barriers to participation: service user involvement in social work training', *Social Work Education*, Vol. 25, No. 4, pp. 385–92

Tyrer, P., Casey, P. and Ferguson, B. (1991) 'Personality disorder in perspective', *British Journal of Psychiatry*, Vol. 159, pp. 463–71

Vodde, R. and Gallant, J. P. (2002) 'Bridging the gap between micro and macro practice: large scale change and a unified model of narrative-deconstructed practice', *Journal of Social Work Education*, Vol. 38, No. 3, pp. 439–58

Waine, B. and Henderson, J. (2003) 'Managers, managing and managerialism', in Henderson, J. and Atkinson, A. (eds) (2003) *Managing Care in Context*, London: Routledge

Warwick, I., Neville, R. and Smith, K. (2006) 'My life in Huddersfield: supporting young asylum seekers and refugees to record their experiences of living in Huddersfield', *Social Work Education*, Vol. 25, No. 2, pp. 129–37

Watson, D. and West, J. (2006) *Social Work Process and Practice: Approaches, Knowledge and Skills*, Basingstoke: Palgrave Macmillan

Webb, S. (2005) *Social Work in a Risk Society: Social and Political Perspectives*, Basingstoke: Palgrave Macmillan

Index